Lostwood National Wildlife Refuge

COMPREHENSIVE CONSERVATION PLAN

December 1998

Prepared by

U.S. Fish and Wildlife Service
Lostwood National Wildlife Refuge
8315 Highway 8
Kenmare, ND 58746

Approved: _____   Date: _____
Acting Regional Director, Region 6, Denver, Colorado

SUBMITTED BY:

Karen A. Smith
Refuge Manager

Date 11/3/98

CONCUR:

Fred G. Giese
Project Leader, Des Lacs NWR Complex

Date 11/5/98

Ronald D. Shupe
Associate Manager, RW/ND/MT

Date 11/10/98

Wilbur N. Ladd, Jr.
Geographic Assistant Regional Director
Northern Ecosystems

Date 11/10/98

Ken McDermond
Programmatic Assistant Regional Director
Refuges and Wildlife

Date 11/10/98

Table of Contents

PREFACE

Often, government plans are mundane, discouraging readers to become involved in the planning process. I thought if I presented, in writing, how dynamic this prairie is, it would encourage you to be involved in planning the future of Lostwood National Wildlife Refuge (Lostwood Refuge). With narration and a few pictures, I present a glimpse of a year on this unique resource so the reader can "experience" the four seasons on Lostwood.

Aerial view of Lostwood National Wildlife Refuge's wetland complexes, one of several prominent resources that makes this Refuge so unique and valuable.

Over every hill lies another wetland or prairie meadow. In between, from hilltop to slough edge, sprawls a most splendid variety of prairie plants.

Four Seasons

*S*pring . . .

Visualize, if you will: you and I standing on a prairie hilltop one crisp early April dawn, looking west across an open expanse of rolling hills covered with last year's plant growth, now a suite of dull tans. Across the hills are patches of snowdrifts on east and south facing slopes, formed by the winter's prevailing, northwesterly winds. Wetlands occur at the bottom of every hill with dense stands of previous years' vegetation still covered in a crusted layer of deep, wind driven snow. Air flowing across our faces is damp and chilly, yet a hint of soft, moist warmth is there, a relief from the relentless, sharp bite of the long, windy arctic blast that can last for six long months. As the sun rises and morning light improves, scattered pastel purples become evident among the dull tan hilltops, the first floral display of the new years' pasque flowers.

About a half mile away a "woo-wooing" sound begins and increases, a cackle erupts, then more, as male sharp-tailed grouse arrive on their dancing grounds to dance relentlessly for their fair ladies. At first, this is the only sound heard, except for the flutter and buzzes of small flocks of longspurs and snow buntings, hurrying to catch up with their earlier migrating fellows.

April progresses, and soon the smaller wetlands begin to thaw. This is an exciting time -- SPRING MIGRA-TION! We walk across the soft soil, loosened by the many thawing ice crystals of winter, and hear a new sound: PINTAILS! whistling, courting, zigzagging, through the softer air. Then mallards. At first, just a pair, but smaller flocks arrive as the day progresses. Hey, what's that yellow speck on the dull tan suite. Wonderful, the first meadowlark has arrived. Meltwater begins to roar in areas where it shouldn't. Snow, melting in warm temperatures, gushes down hills into dry coulees, turning them into a white-water stream for a day or two. The wetlands fill, their ice rising and softening. Wetland edges become open water. Between these edges of spring and winter, diving ducks appear, purring and gurgling songs to their accompanying ladies. The large lakes have not been released from winter's grip, but the dark honeycomb cover promises that soon winter's hold will be relinquished.

Those hills, now with a hint of green showing, have so much life, it is difficult to hear sharp-tails dancing, even on still, early morns: giant Canada geese honk, mallards quack, migrating sparrows' whistle and chip, pipits' skylark, meadowlarks' flute, and the "noise" increases. Spring tries hard to push winter away, driving the cold north with strong, gusty southerly winds more gentle to the face, but winter does not give up easily and returns with strong, sharp-biting, northerly winds. Eventually old-man winter loses, spring prevails, and new life abounds.

Sounds multiply as more life arrives in May. The sky resonates, evidence of something always moving: skeins of snow, white-fronted, and smaller Canada geese and ducks, flittering sparrows and warblers, kettling sandhill cranes, darting yellowlegs, winnowing snipe, and, dropping in from nowhere, clowning coots. Sprinting through in small flocks, just above the rolling terrain, we hear small flocks of shorebirds. Some land along exposed beaches to rest and feed, but most don't stop: the relentless urge of migration never lets them rest. Harriers drift through: some stay, most float on by, the males sometimes "sky-dancing" perhaps to impress females along the way.

Flocks of ruddy ducks appear as rafts on opened lakes. Western and eared grebes are heard there too.

May explodes with migrating and nesting birds, all here at the same time. Then it happens again: the north wind returns, stronger than ever, biting, driving a heavy, wet snow. Food is covered. Early arrivals are caught: some make it, some do not. But just as quick as winter returned, spring rushes back.

More grass-loving sparrows arrive using melodious songs to establish territories. Sprague's pipits, territories well established, skylark for hours over ridges and hilltops. Life is good. More early colors are displayed, such as plains cymopterus, but these are not very bold, perhaps too bashful to display brilliance so early. But the green is persisting, as well as more colorful flowers: cushion milk-vetch, golden-bean, early yellow locoweed, prairie buttercup. Now wetlands are filled with water and life: blackbirds, both yellow-headed and red-winged, create continuous raucous; ducks battle on water and in the air to retain territories. Soon, duck pairs are walking around on uplands, searching for THE nest site, but flush by our presence, complaining loudly and persistently while flying in tight circles, directly overhead. A coyote yips and barks at us, unaccustomed to observing humans after the long winter months.

A variety of "peeps" are along most lake shorelines, feeding intensely before they continue their migration northward. Suddenly this peaceful scene explodes and out of nowhere a charcoal streak stoops through the flushing shorebirds — PEREGRINE!

May gives way to June. We are now walking in a lush growth of grasses and flowers. Birds are singing all around us, some so loud, like the continuous, bubbling flight song of the bobolink, that it prevents us from hearing the more subtle song of the Le Conte's sparrow. Chestnut-collared longspur's make their presence known on grazed, rocky ridge tops with their pleasant, rapid, buzzy warble. Upland sandpipers are wolf-whistling on previous years' burns. Baird's sparrows abound: their melodious song, combines with others to produce an impromptu prairie orchestra.

The last to arrive, sounding like a rusty gate swinging in the wind, is the sharp-tailed sparrow. This completes the prairie nesters' arrival. Now everyone is busy maintaining territories, nesting, and taking care of newly-hatched young.

We roam across the hills, not far from a big saline lake that's so salty it can be tasted in the wind, when a marbled godwit explodes from a short-vegetated hilltop, and relentlessly dives at our heads to drive us from her nest. We walk away from this site so as not to disturb her anymore, only to have a subtle hooting sound approach. A Wilson's phalarope is afraid we will come too near his nest. So, we again move away, this time closer to the white shoreline of the saline lake only to have a distinct "peep-lo" sound draw closer. This time it is a piping plover coming to express its displeasure of our presence. Everywhere we turn, something flushes, gives alarm, scolds, or sings proudly. Life is so full, it is difficult to be conscious of the individual because the whole is so overwhelming.

Summer...

Color abounds everywhere now. Brilliant red prairie lilies line the wetland edges, and a deep, iridescent purple of two-grooved milkvetch is found nearby in large, round bunches. On the hill above us, sunny spots of Gaillardia wave to-and-fro in the summer breeze. Fleabanes' hairlike ray petals bloom in pastel pinks. Butterflies, some blue, some white, some orange, flutter about. Sounds abound too, not only from birds, but from insects, all contributing to a resounding prairie orchestra. So many things are happening, it is difficult to slow down and "smell the flowers," or to take time to watch the evening hilltops reflect a golden green from the warm, setting sun, contrasting with the dark green, shadowed slopes. June rushes by; too beautiful and astounding to absorb in just 30 days.

Soon, needlegrass seeds are maturing, reflecting the sun's rays in sparkling crystals as the gentle summer breezes sway them to-and-fro. As the seeds mature, entire hilltops turn to a waving sea of gold. Mingled in this golden sea are a variety of pinks: purple coneflower, purple prairie clover, spotted gayfeather. In richer soil sites, warm-season grasses become showy, such as big bluestem pushing up its dark green, stiff seed stalk mixed with hints of deep purple. Prairie dropseed sends up its wispy, delicate panicum of dotted seeds. Flowers on these richer sites are very iridescent, particularly the luminous purple of blazing star. Plant life abounds, of many species, because several different plant communities meet here ranging from the tallgrass prairie of the east to the arid prairie of the west. While we are so absorbed in the luxurious plant community around us, we suddenly become aware that the courting and territorial sounds of June are waning. Now, more insect sounds are heard, and bird sounds are softer, shorter notes of parents feeding young and scolding us when we press too close to their family affairs. Ducklings are now getting quite large, looking more like their moms each day.

July has slipped by, but how, where did it go? Time moves so fast.

Tall, white billows appear on the west horizon. Very pretty. They build into massive, towering giants as they move closer. Western skies darken except for white streaks flashing continuously. Blue skies overhead have given way to rumbling and darkness, then flashes of bold light from the atmosphere to the ground. Rain begins, pours, water rushes everywhere. Something hard and small hits the ground and bounces two feet back into the air. HAIL! The air turns white with hail. Rain once again, or is it a vertical river? On the west horizon, blue sky! The storm passes and sun shines through millions of droplets, fields of diamonds sprinkled across the prairie.

Days are hot now. Winds, recently soft and gentle to the skin, bite again, but now like sandpaper. The hilltops turn to cream color, but still are sprinkled with color, particularly blues and yellows of asters and yellows of goldenrods. In rich soil sites, grasses begin to turn pastel pinks, purples, oranges, reds, yellows while native shrubs turn sharp reds, oranges, and yellows.

Green still hangs in there, but it is scattered, mostly in prairie cordgrass. Red dots, from prairie rose hips, are scattered on hilltops. The once spectacular flowers are replaced with pastel-colored seed heads that spatter the sun's rays.

Fall...

It is eerily silent on the hilltop! Where have all the birds gone? Only sounds of grasshoppers and crickets prevail. Ah, let's move to the wetlands. But, what has happened? Many are dry, but look, over there, there's water! Water birds abound--ducks, coots, grebes, soras, sharp-tailed sparrows, blackbirds, dragonflies, midges--yes, bountiful life is still present.

As this bountiful life dwindles, new life begins to appear-- migration is on. First are the tundra nesting shorebirds, lingering along mudflats and shorelines to feed and drift about. But all too soon, many of these move on, leaving behind mostly waterfowl, those that reproduced here. By the end of August, even most of these move north to molt and feed, a process known as staging, leaving the prairie quite silent. These waterfowl, and those produced further north, do not return for several weeks, unless some sudden, mid-October storm pushes them by us without even saying good-bye.

It's September, and the rolling prairie hills reflect fall colors in the grasses, forbs, and shrubs. It is a subtle beauty only lasting for a few days, a contrast to the arrogant fall colors of deciduous forests, a softness pleasing to the eye: creams, pinks, and pastel oranges, purples, and yellows.

New sounds overhead! A raucous, trumpeting rattle is heard. We look up to see migrating sandhill cranes in long, v-shaped strings, rising up and down on air currents, then suddenly catching an updraft, and rapidly kettling to 5,000 feet. As the day progresses, some cranes land and feed on grazed or burned areas, or settle onto mudflats and shallow bays of large lakes to night roost. This crane activity continues through fall, sometimes in small, drifting flocks, sometimes in major migration thrusts.

One day while walking across the hilltops in warm, unusually calm weather, we notice dots of circling movements overhead. On rising kettles, large groups of Swainson's hawks are on the move, drifting southward effortlessly by the dozens. Late in the day, some drop and begin hopping on the ground, hunting grasshoppers. More sparing hawks, falcons, and accipiters move through, along with the whistles and chips of migrating sparrows and juncos, although not as musical as in the spring. Soon most of the sandhills have passed through, as have most raptor and songbird species.

We wait, wait for the gradual, but sometimes quite sudden explosion of migrating waterfowl that signals fall's close. At first, it is just one "v" here, another over there, of geese, mostly white-fronts. But, a few days later, the raucous of snow goose flocks pierce the air. Resident giant Canada geese, seem to dislike the commotion that accompanies large flocks of snow geese, leave the preferred lakes to quieter, open-water wetlands. Accompanying the mass of snow geese are the symbol of the United States, bald eagles. These eagles continually test the flocks for a goose not quite fit for the long trip south. Golden eagles partake as well, but usually show up later, just before freeze-up.

W*inter* . . .

The air now is unsettled. Winds constantly shift from gentle southerlies to harsh northerlies. Sometimes the shifts are light, sometimes of hurricane force. Standing on the same hilltop as we did in spring, we see dark gray clouds being driven in, their tops and bottoms sheared by sharp winds. The rolling darkness approaches; snow falls. Ducks and geese linger, continue to feed in nearby grain stubble fields. The storm passes. Warm, sunny days return. These are quiet days, with soft winds, and a few chip notes of passing warblers and sparrows that are a little behind schedule. Ducks and geese continue to field-feed and roost on large lakes. It's the end of October. We can feel it. They clearly feel it. They are more restless than ever. You can see it in their flight

behavior. They search for a good field to feed in but are not satisfied when they land. They lift, bounce around in the increasing winds, land again. Feed a little, spook, and lift again, and struggle into the howling wind to the next field. Overhead, high overhead, pass skein after skein of waterfowl, sometimes only visible with binoculars. We see the major fall migration taking place; they are not taking time to say good-bye this year. The birds on the ground become even more restless. After feeding till dark, they return to the lakes, fighting winds more than 40 mph. Temperatures plummet! Single digits! The next morning we arise from our night's sleep. Winds are relentless. The LAKES, frozen, and, BIRDS, gone!

After three days of relentless, cold, piercing winds, a mild winter day begins in light winds and double digit temperatures. Once in a while, a small flock of geese or ducks are observed, but, otherwise, all is very quiet. A few juncos and tree sparrows still chip here and there, but silence is becoming the norm.

The last harriers drift by us. Rough-legged hawks appear, hovering like sparrow hawks while hunting for mice. Gray clouds are heavy in the northwest. Snow arrives, falls, and builds. Winds pick up, driving the snow into new locations and shapes. Even though December and January are filled with lots of sunshine, it brings little warmth to the snow, allowing winds to constantly reshape it. It is silent, except for the wind!

It is a cold, still morn. Longspurs and snow buntings appear in large, bouncing flocks as they roll across the stark, prairie hills blanketed in white. A sound, like a knife cutting through cold, still air, is heard-- a sharp-tailed grouse appears overhead, then another and another, heading somewhere to feed before returning to day-roost in the snow. Storms come and go, some so severe that resident wildlife, like white-tailed deer and great-horned owls, find it tough to get enough to eat. Cold, wind, and snow takes its toll.

Warmth from the sun grows. We can feel it. The winds do not bite as they did. The snow cover melts on the surface, forming a crust thick enough on which to cross-country ski--oh, what fun! It is too warm, it is 50°F; the snow is melting too fast, making the skiing poor, but oh, how good the warmth feels to us. It is a mistake to feel too warm--the gray northwest skies warn us of impending cold, wind, and snow. It dumps on us and blows it into deep drifts, especially on east- and south-facing hillsides. The storm passes. Flocks of snow buntings and longspurs pass by, with sprinkles of horned larks singing the first spring songs. March is here. Spring is not far away. It has been a good winter, most resident wildlife survived, and abundant snow is available to refill wetlands and restore topsoil moisture that will produce lush plant growth and lots of insects for nesting birds.

Life is **good**. **NO**, it is more than good. Life is unbeliev-ably beautiful with its ever-changing seasons and bounty. Such is one year, four seasons, on Lostwood National Wildlife Refuge.

INTRODUCTION AND BACKGROUND

Purpose and Need for a Plan

"As the century nears its end and demand for food and competition for land escalate, a most important issue facing conservationists will be the preservation of a mosaic of habitats in which can be preserved a representative cross-section of native species" (Samson and Knopf 1982).

Preserving such habitat mosaics provides beautiful, natural areas, but without intimate involvement of the United States citizen, many of these habitats may be lost or inappropriately cared for due to lack of support. John C. Sawhill, President and Chief Executive Officer of The Nature Conservancy, wrote:

"By conserving and celebrating important natural areas, we can provide the necessary platform of beautiful, unspoiled places critical to building a more intimate relationship between people and land ... From that intimacy will come the connectedness--the sense of interdependence--with nature that so many of us crave. Similarly, the more places we save, the greater the opportunity to inspire wonder and commitment in people. And ultimately, ... that will decide the fate of the natural world" (Sawhill 1996).

The Draft Comprehensive Conservation (Management) Plan was written in accordance with a Refuge System policy requiring "all lands of the National Wildlife Refuge System will be managed in accordance with an approved Comprehensive Management Plan that will guide management decisions and set forth strategies for achieving refuge unit purposes." The National Wildlife Refuge Improvement Act of 1997 (passed in October) changes this from a policy to law, and calls the plans Comprehensive Conservation Plan (CCP).

This Comprehensive Conservation Plan has had public comment, and we have incorporated those comments someplace in this Plan. Hopefully public involvement will not end here but will continue, further developing an intimate relationship between the people and Lostwood Refuge, a beautiful mixed-grass prairie nestled in northwestern North Dakota. The Plan presents a conservation direction for the mission and goals of the Refuge System and Lostwood Refuge. Remember, this Plan is just one step, part of a continuing Adaptive Resource Management philosophy, a philosophy essential to incorporate new directions and knowledge as they develop to conserve and preserve Lostwood Refuge as a unique natural resource.

Hopefully, through this continuing planning process, appropriate revenue and staffing can be achieved for Lostwood Refuge. The result will be a healthy, mixed-grass prairie, and a much needed, well-developed, public use program including environmental education and interpretation, hunting, wildlife observation and photography, and other compatible wildlife-dependent recreational activities. The Refuge System is required to "... ensure that the biological integrity and environmental health of the Refuge System is maintained for the benefit of present and future generations of Americans" (Executive Order 12996, March 25, 1996), which incorporates managing a natural resource to maintain its health and provide recreational opportunities for the public, all at the same time. This is a challenging task, so the complexity involved in this Plan is evident. We need your help. Please take time to review and become involved in planning the future of one of our national treasures, Lostwood Refuge.

National Wildlife Refuge System

Mission

The National Wildlife Refuge System is a diverse collection of 512 refuges encompassing over 92 million acres, spanning all states and several territories. The National Wildlife Refuge System Improvement Act of 1997 gives the Refuge System's mission:

"To administer a national network of lands and waters for the conservation, management, and where appropriate, restoration of the fish, wildlife, and plant resources and their habitats within the United States for the benefit of present and future generations of Americans."

The Act establishes a Refuge System policy that "each refuge shall be managed to fulfill the mission of the Refuge System, as well as the specific purposes for which that refuge was established." The Act establishes a hierarchy among refuge activities: that first are activities to meet refuge purposes and Refuge System Mission; second is to facilitate compatible wildlife dependent recreation. By default, other uses would be the last priority.

The National Wildlife Refuge System differs from other federally-owned lands, (i.e., National Forest Service, Bureau of Land Management, or National Park Service) in that wildlife conservation, not multiple-use activities, is the fundamental mission. Wildlife and wildlife conservation come first over public use activities. The Act further recognizes and encourages public use activities centering around wildlife-dependent recreational uses. Even these must be compatible with the mission of the Refuge System and individual refuge purposes, but the Act strongly encourages facilitation of these activities if compatible. Wildlife-dependent recreational uses include hunting, fishing, wildlife observation and photography, and environmental education and interpretation.

The Refuge Improvement Act explicitly defines words to guide the Refuge System. Some definitions are presented here to help the reader understand what specific phrases mean.

"The term 'compatible use' means a wildlife-dependent recreational use or any other use of a refuge that, in the sound professional judgement of the Director, will not materially interfere with or detract from the fulfillment of the mission of the Refuge System or the purposes of the refuge."

The terms 'wildlife-dependent recreation' and 'wildlife-dependent recreational use' mean a use of a refuge involving hunting, fishing, wildlife observation and photography, or environmental education and interpretation."

"The term 'sound professional judgment' means a finding, determination, or decision that is consistent with principles of sound fish and wildlife management and administration, available science and resources, and adherence to the requirements of the Act and other applicable laws."

"The terms 'purposes of the refuge' and 'purpose of each refuge' mean the purposes specified in or derived from the law, proclamation, executive order, agreement, public land order, donation document, or administrative memorandum establishing, authorizing, or expanding a refuge, refuge unit, or refuge subunit."

Goals and guiding principles of the National Wildlife Refuge System (Refuge System) identified in the 1997 Executive Order, 12996, are:

Goals

A.   To preserve, restore, and enhance, in their natural ecosystem (when practicable), all species of animals and plants that are endangered or threatened with becoming endangered.

B.   Perpetuate the migratory bird resource.

C.   Preserve a natural diversity and abundance of fauna and flora on refuge lands.

D.   To provide an understanding and appreciation of fish and wildlife ecology and man's role in his environment, and to provide refuge visitors with high quality, safe, wholesome, and enjoyable activities compatible with the purposes for which the refuge was established.

Guiding Principles

Public Use. The Refuge System provides important opportunities for compatible wildlife-dependent recreational activities involving hunting, fishing, wildlife observation and photography, and environmental education and interpretation.

Habitat. Fish and wildlife will not prosper without high-quality habitat, and without fish and wildlife, traditional uses of refuges cannot be sustained. The Refuge System will continue to conserve and enhance the quality and diversity of fish and wildlife habitat within refuges.

Partnerships. America's sportsmen and women were the first partners who insisted on protecting valuable wildlife habitat within wildlife refuges. Conservation partnerships with other Federal agencies, State agencies, tribes, organizations, industry, and the general public can make significant contributions to the growth and management of the Refuge System.

Public Involvement. The public should be given a full and open opportunity to participate in decisions regarding acquisition and management of our National Wildlife Refuges.

Regulatory Statutes

Other legal mandates and policy guidelines of the Refuge System that also affect Lostwood Refuge are:

". . . for use as an inviolate sanctuary, or for any other management purpose, for migratory birds." (16 U.S.C. § 715d , Migratory Bird Conservation Act)

". . . the conservation of the wetlands of the Nation in order to maintain the public benefits they provide and to help fulfill international obligations contained in various migratory bird treaties and conventions . . ." (16 U.S.C. § 3901[b], 100 Stat. 3583, Emergency Wetlands Resources Act of 1986)

". . . review every roadless area of 5,000 contiguous acres or more and every roadless island, regardless of size, within the National Wildlife Refuge System . . . and report to the President of the United States his recommendations as to the suitability or nonsuitability of each such area or island for preservation of wilderness." (The Wilderness Act, Public Law 88-577)

". . . the following lands are hereby designated as wilderness and, therefore, as components of the national wilderness preservation system: . . . certain lands in the Lostwood National Wildlife Refuge, North Dakota, . . ." (To Designate Certain Lands as Wilderness. January 3, 1975. Public Law 93-632)

". . .the Federal land manager and the Federal official charged with direct responsibility for management of Class I areas shall have an affirmative responsibility to protect all those air quality related values (including visibility) of any such lands." (Clean Air Act section 165(d)(2)(B))

Lostwood National Wildlife Refuge

Purpose and Regulatory Statutes

Lostwood Refuge is "... a refuge and breeding ground for migratory birds and other wildlife ..." (Executive Order 7171-A, September 4, 1935). Located in northwestern North Dakota, it is primarily a breeding ground for migratory birds during spring and summer.

Lush prairie wetlands help create the unique diversity of habitat on Lostwood Refuge that makes the area so attractive to a variety of breeding migratory birds.

In 1975, the 5,577-acre Lostwood Wilderness Area was established within the boundaries of Lostwood Refuge (P.L. 88-577). Its importance was described in the Final EIS, "A unique example of the Coteau du Missouri of the northern Great Plains would be set aside within our Nation that constitutes the last sizeable tract of this interesting formation." The area is designated as Class I and, therefore, receives the highest protection under the Clean Air Act. In 1995, An interagency Wilderness Strategic Plan was signed by the Directors of Bureau of Land Management, National Park Service, U.S. Fish and Wildlife Service, and Chief of the U.S. Forest Service. This Plan is designed "To secure the benefits of wilderness as called for in the Wilderness Act, ... Management actions are identified and grouped into five broad topics. While some of these actions are more general than others, and they all may not be equally important to each of our agencies, our commitment to progress in every one of these areas is unequivocal. America's 'enduring resource of wilderness' is too important for anything less." Those five topics are listed below.

1) Preservation of natural and biological values

2) Management of social values

3) Administrative policy and interagency coordination

4) Training of agency personnel

5) Public awareness and understanding

Establishment and History

In the late 1800's, the area known today as Lostwood Refuge was mixed-grass prairie mainly a wheatgrass-needlegrass community, with almost no trees and few shrubs (Coupland 1950, 1961; Singh *et al.* 1983). It was a wide open prairie with nothing to block the vista of rolling, sodded horizon. Migratory birds from ducks to sparrows were the most visible wildlife, but sharp-tailed grouse, a hardy resident species, were common. Few species of small mammals, and even fewer of amphibians and reptiles were present, perhaps owing to the harsh, prolonged winters of this northern climate. Invertebrates, adapted to frequent and periodic drought and vegetation removal mainly by bison herds and fire, also were abundant and active during the growing season.

Teeming abundance of migratory birds, spring through fall, was the main appeal in establishing Lostwood as a National Wildlife Refuge. Numerous wetlands, all types and shapes formed by the Wisconsin glacier some 10,000 years ago, provided prime habitat for many species of water-dependent birds. Within wetlands during wet years, grebes, ducks, and giant Canada geese proliferated—abundance and variety of duck species present in this area were main incentives in establishing Lostwood Refuge. The habitat between wetlands and upland grasslands provided breeding habitat for another group of birds, species with restricted distribution such as marbled godwit, piping plover, sharp-tailed sparrow. Unique upland birds, some with restricted breeding ranges, were common on the upland prairie: Baird's sparrow, Sprague's pipit, clay-colored sparrow, chestnut-collared longspur, upland sandpiper. Using the entire prairie ecosystem were other unique prairie birds, the Swainson's hawk and, with a more limited breeding range, the ferruginous hawk and burrowing owl. The Refuge System was also interested in the area's fall migrant use. Geese, swans, ducks, and sandhill cranes annually stopped at Lostwood Refuge for a short rest during their southward migration.

Murphy (1993) reviewed and summarized historical accounts of early explorers and naturalists who traveled through the area, and found that, in the early- and mid-1800's, the Coteau prairie of northwestern North Dakota was covered with short grasses, or barren, wherever recent fire and especially bison occurred which apparently were most places (i.e., Coues, Clandening, in Murphy 1993). These observations supported a view that the region was, historically, in a more arid, short grass state (reviewed in Murphy 1993). But, early explorers' and naturalists' accounts also implied periodic deferment or rest from heavy grazing and fire, during which grasses would recover. Frequent mention was made by these authors that woody vegetation needed for cooking fires was scarce on the Missouri Coteau. Later records from surveyors' and biologists' notes in the late 1800's and early 1900's confirmed such observations, that present-day Lostwood Refuge historically was grass prairie. Aspen reached tree stage only after several decades of fire suppression that accompanied settlement by persons of European origin. Historical records and indirect evidence from Lostwood Refuge reported in

Murphy (op. cit.) also corroborated a 5-10 year fire frequency for the region, asserted by Wright and Bailey (1982).

R. Kellogg (Smithsonian Inst., Archives Record Unit 7176) gave one of the best, concise historical descriptions of the area in August 1915:

" ... This region is high prairie country. Numerous lakes, marshes and meadows are scattered over the country. The prairie is rolling and in some places very hilly. The subsoil in a lot of places is from a foot to a foot and a half of gravel. The only timber in this region was formerly on the southeast corner of [Lower] Lostwood Lake but this was cut off by the homesteaders and now there is nothing left but small oak [sic] and poplar brush, with a clump of willows here and there."

As immigrant settlement of northwestern North Dakota took place at the beginning of the twentieth century, mixed-grass prairies were replaced by grain fields. Wetlands were drained to enhance agricultural production. Even though drainage and other wetland-decimating factors have taken their toll elsewhere in the state, prairie wetlands are still prominent on the Missouri Coteau in northwestern North Dakota.

The Lostwood Refuge area was homesteaded mainly during 1910-1930, with some native sod broken and planted to small grain crops. When Lostwood Refuge lands were first purchased in 1935, about 75 percent of the designated Refuge area remained as unbroken (native) mixed-grass prairie. In the absence of fire with settlement, woody species rapidly expanded to dominate Lostwood Refuge's upland habitats, with snowberry covering greater than 50 percent of uplands and most of the Refuge changing from a mixed-grass prairie to aspen parkland by the mid-1980's (Murphy 1993). With this significant change in plant community, so too did the wildlife community dramatically change. Many grassland birds unique to this area disappeared from the Lostwood Refuge or became very scarce.

Cultural Resources

Lostwood Refuge lies within a relatively un-researched archaeological area. The nearest site that has been excavated and studied is the Long Creek site near Estevan, Saskatchewan, about 40 miles northwest of the Lostwood Refuge (Wettlaufer and Mayer-Oakes 1960). That site revealed occupation of the area as long ago as 5000 years ago. Because of the close proximity of Lostwood Refuge to the Long Creek site, some of the same cultures also may have occurred in the Lostwood area. Historical records indicate that the last inhabitants of the area before Western European settlement were the southern Assiniboian tribes (Denig 1961), who now reside in Canada. At least 200 "tipi ring" sites are known to exist on Lostwood Refuge where Native Americans occupied the area either in permanent or transient camps.

The Service's Regional Archaeologist will be consulted during the planning phase of any proposed project and will determine the need for a cultural resource inventory in consultation with the North Dakota Historic Preservation Office.

Planning Issues and Opportunities

A planning issue is any unsettled matter that requires a management decision; i.e., a Service initiative, an opportunity, a management problem, a potential threat to the resources of the unit, a conflict in uses, a public concern, or the presence of an undesirable resource condition. Input on issues was sought from the public, Federal, State and local agencies, private organizations, and political entities through an Environmental Assessment and associated public comment period, and the draft Comprehensive Conservation Plan (previously called Comprehensive Management Plan).

Scoping for planning issues began with the 1994 Environmental Assessment (EA) entitled "Management of Upland Habitats on Lostwood National Wildlife Refuge." Scoping is a process Lostwood Refuge used whereby Federal, State and local agencies, political entities, and private organizations were sent copies and invited to participate in the early planning of an EA to assist the Service in identifying issues and alternative management actions to be considered and evaluated in the EA. Letters announcing the availability of the draft EA were sent to all members of the Lostwood Communication Council (a local group of citizens interested in Lostwood Refuge's management and other Service programs). News releases announced availability of the draft EA for review during a 30-day comment period (June 6 - July 6, 1994) were published in local and regional newspapers. Only one letter was received regarding the draft EA from the public during or after the comment period. That letter supported the preferred alternative, "Enhanced Management Alternative."

Within the spirit and intent of the Council on Environmental Quality's regulations for implementing the National Environmental Policy Act (NEPA) and other statutes, orders, and policies that protect fish and wildlife resources, it was determined that actions within the "Management of Upland Habitats on Lostwood National Wildlife Refuge" EA were found to have no significant negative environmental effects. A copy of the "Finding of No Significant Impact" of the EA is in Appendix C. A copy of the EA's "Compatibility Determination" is in Appendix C.

Public involvement with Lostwood Refuge's Draft Comprehensive Conservation Plan was through news releases, a public comment period, (August 25 to September 30, 1997), and a public meeting (September 17, 1997 in Stanley, North Dakota). The issues, concerns, and opportunities presented here include comments from interested citizens and Service personnel. It is only after all issues, concerns, and opportunities are identified and clearly understood that the planning process can fully be utilized. Lostwood Refuge's management strategies, along with accompanying goals and objectives, will address these issues in some manner, unless otherwise noted.

Land Acquisition

A common local concern was future acquisition within the approved boundary established in the 1935 Executive Order that created Lostwood Refuge. Opposition to further acquisition existed because it was viewed as lost opportunity for local farm and ranch operations and lost tax revenues for local governments.

Hunting

Some citizens wanted more of Lostwood Refuge open to upland game hunting during September - October. Lostwood Refuge currently has a split upland game season, one before the deer gun season begins, and one after the deer gun season ends. About 4,600 acres are open during the early season, and the entire Refuge (except around Refuge headquarters) is open to upland game hunting during the late season. The opportunity exists to open other portions of the Refuge during the first season through the compatibility determination procedure.

Some local citizens were concerned that reduction in size and number of aspen clumps may have negative effects for white-tailed deer.

Class I Air Quality

Concerns were expressed about the potential conflict that may arise between habitat renovation and maintenance through the use of prescribed burning and the Clean Air Act requirements for Lostwood Refuge and Class I area of the Lostwood Wilderness Area. The use of prescribed burning must be carefully balanced against requirements of the Clean Air Act to protect and enhance air quality in the Refuge and Class I air quality of the Lostwood Wilderness Area. When noncompliance is identified, the Refuge will identify solutions and comply with all requirements. The Interagency Wilderness Strategic Plan, completed by the Bureau of Land Management, National Park Service, U.S. Fish and Wildlife Service, and U.S. Forest Service, identified that without management of natural values of wilderness areas, the underlying fabric of the National Wilderness Preservation System is at risk. One of the identified strategies is to restore fire to its natural role in the ecosystem, allowing flexible spending of fire funding to cover prescribed fire.

Wildlife-oriented Recreation

Some expressed appreciation of current horseback riding opportunities on Lostwood Refuge.

Environmental Education and Interpretation

Almost no funds or permanent staffing are available to accomplish the Refuge System's goals for compatible recreation and outreach. Potential conflict exists between developing permanent public use facilities (i.e., interpretative trails) and Refuge management needs. Limitations on fire and grazing would cause habitat quality to decline for indigenous wildlife. Interpretative facilities may show only degraded, mismanaged prairie.

Disability

Some expressed the Americans With Disabilities Act of 1992 needs inclusion in Goals and Objectives. The Refuge System will fully comply with the Disability Act.

Wildlife and Habitat Management

Habitat needs conflict among some indigenous species. For example, Dakota skipper (an endemic tallgrass prairie species) may need long-term rest to complete a successful life cycle, while Baird's sparrow, a species of concern in northern mixed-grass prairie, needs only 2-4 years of rest after a prescribed burn or grazing period but declines significantly with any additional rest.

A potential conflict exists between introduction of certain species identified in the Endangered Species goal, i.e., western burrowing owl, and with other species needs, i.e., vegetation structure needed by Baird's sparrow, Sprague's pipit, and waterfowl.

If Lostwood Refuge must rely strongly on partnerships to secure funds, a program that takes a tremendous amount of time, the resource will be compromised because less staff time is available to maintain " . . . the critical biological integrity and environmental health . . ." of the Refuge, so strongly emphasized in Executive Order 12996 and the Refuge Improvement Act.

RESOURCE AND REFUGE DESCRIPTION

Ecosystem Setting and Description

The 26,904-acre Lostwood Refuge is in Burke and Mountrail Counties in northwestern North Dakota, 23 miles south of Canada and 70 miles east of Montana (see Maps 1 and 2). It lies within the 12- to 19-mile wide Missouri Coteau, a physiographic region chiefly of moderate (100-200 feet) relief, dead ice moraine deposited by the Wisconsin glacier over a previously occurring escarpment (Clayton 1967; Freers 1973; Bluemle 1977). Its rolling topography (elevation 2,227-2,442 feet) is interspersed with 5,381 acres of prairie wetlands (20 percent of Refuge area) of all types and sizes. Hummocky, knob-and-kettle topography typical of the Missouri Coteau consists almost entirely of nonintegrated drainage; rainfall and snowmelt collect in wetland basins via surface runoff and subsurface seepage (LaBaugh 1986; Winter 1989). Presence of glacial till (Coleharbor formation) is evidenced by erratic and thin, gravelly, mostly loam soils. The far southern 5 mi² of Lostwood Refuge has numerous deep, brushy coulees that drain into a 0.9-mi² saline lake.

The climate at Lostwood Refuge is semiarid with normal temperature extremes of -40°F in winter and 100°F in summer. Mean annual precipitation is 16.6 inches, with extremes of 9 to 29 inches. Some winters have almost no snow, while others are severe with snowstorms from October through May. May and June are normally the wettest months, while July and August present violent thunderstorms often accompanied with several inches of rain or hail. Winds ranging from 5-20 mph are prevalent through most seasons, and 30-40 mph winds are common, particularly in spring and fall. All wetlands, except major lakes, may be completely full one year and completely dry 5-10 years later. These extreme conditions create a "boom and bust" scenario for the production of water-dependent species such as ducks. This wet-to dry-cycle also prevents frequent disease outbreaks (i.e., botulism) and provides for maximum wetland fertility, and thus high water bird productivity, in wet years (Kantrud *et al.* 1989). The growing season varies from 90 to 100 days.

Primary soils are Zahl-Williams and Zahl-Max loams, characterized as thinly developed, well-drained, fine loamy soil complexes, on 3-25 percent slopes. On hilltops and upper slopes, Zahl loam makes up 60 percent of the Zahl-Max complex; on lower slopes, Max loams comprise 25-50 percent of this complex. Spring surface runoff can be rapid on steep slopes when sudden warm temperatures melt snowdrifts. The hazard of wind and water erosion is severe on cultivated areas during any season.

When Refuge lands were first purchased in 1935, about 75 percent of uplands on the designated Refuge area remained unbroken (native), mixed-grass prairie. Although dominated by needle and wheat grasses, it included a unique array of plant communities from dry hilltops to slopes to moist sites (Appendix K for list of dominant plant species). This prairie landscape abounded with diverse, abundant native wildlife communities. Upland habitats were characterized by Baird's sparrow, Sprague's pipit along with numerous other grassland dependent birds. Wetland edge habitats contained marbled godwit, piping plover, Nelson's sharp-tailed sparrow, and others. Wetlands abounded with ducks and other water-dependent species.

The last free-ranging bison in North Dakota occurred in the early 1880's (Hornaday 1889; Grinell 1970; Joyce and Skold 1988). The last raging wildfires occurred in the early 1900's as persons of European descent home-steaded on the Missouri Coteau of northwestern North Dakota in the early 1900's, where Lostwood Refuge is located (reviewed by Murphy 1993). Before settlement, early explorers conveyed that no trees or shrubs were anywhere (reviewed by Murphy 1993). However, suckers and saplings of quaking aspen apparently were scattered over the prairie, but were dwarfed by frequent fire and herbivore grazing. Although no trees existed on Lostwood Refuge before settlement (except for an elm grove along a Refuge lake), by 1938, aspen tree clumps totaled 275 and covered 100 acres; by 1969, 500 clumps totaling 375 acres; and in 1985, 540 clumps (475 acres), or about 13 clumps/mi² (Murphy 1993). The spread has

Lostwood Refuge's plant diversity on moist soil sites includes components of the tallgrass prairie.

Lostwood Refuge's plant diversity on dry soil sites includes components of the mixed-grass prairie and short-grass of the more arid west.

continued, except on areas with several prescribed burns. Most clumps border wetlands, particularly seasonal wetlands. Over time, these clumps spread around the wetlands, then invade the wetland basin. By 1985, more than 300 wetlands were overtaken by aspen on Lostwood Refuge (USFWS, unpubl. data).

Other woody expansion took place too, particularly on uplands where a low-growing shrub, western snowberry, gradually increased. Lack of reference to low brush in historical accounts suggests the plant either was inconspicuous or occurred infrequently before settlement. An estimate of 5 percent small shrub composition comprised by snowberry and other low brush in pristine mixed-grass prairie has been proffered based on relict sites (summarized by Murphy 1993). Snowberry has been found to proliferate under fire suppression and cattle grazing (summarized in Murphy 1993). Land use from the early 1900's to mid-1970's was primarily livestock grazing and purposely excluded fire. Each designated unit was grazed from annual season-long grazing for 30-40 years to zero years (long-term rest or idle treatment). Comparing the two extremes in treatment, little difference in plant composition resulted with both having extensive invasion extremes in woody plants and exotic grasses. Aerial photographs, taken in 1935, reveal snowberry already covering 24 percent of the upland native prairie, and by 1985, the extent of snowberry-dominated cover doubled. This trend parallels that of aspen proliferation.

Not only are unburned native plant communities at Lostwood Refuge becoming dominated by woody plants, associated changes in the wildlife community are showing. One of the most conspicuous of these changes is within the raptor community, a group of species sensitive to alterations in the food chain and habitat structure (Newton 1979). Historically (ca. late 1800's to early 1900's), Swainson's and ferruginous hawks, true grassland raptors, were dominant breeders, while great-horned owls were uncommon and red-tailed hawks absent as breeding species on Lostwood Refuge (Murphy 1993). But with the advance of aspen trees, great-horned owls and red-tailed hawks increased and pioneered, respectively, and by the 1970s were dominant, large raptors on the Refuge. Swainson's hawks are now uncommon, nesting only on the Refuge periphery, and at most only one pair of ferruginous hawks nest on the Refuge. The same transition of grassland to parkland, with the raptor community changing from Swainson's and ferruginous hawks (true grassland raptors) to red-tailed hawks and great horned owls (generalist raptors), has been observed in southern Saskatchewan (Houston and Bechard 1983, 1984) and Alberta (Schmutz 1984). Another conspicuous change is within the grassland passerine community, a group of species sensitive to vegetation structure and composition. Madden (1996) studied 10 upland passerine species on burned and unburned areas of Lostwood Refuge. On unburned areas, Baird's sparrow, grasshopper sparrow, Le Conte's sparrow, Sprague's pipit, and western meadowlark were never detected on unburned areas, and bobolinks were rarely detected. These species, however, were commonly found on areas treated with fire, as were two grassland-generalist species (brown-headed cowbird and savannah sparrow), and two shrub-associated species (clay-colored sparrow and common yellowthroat).

On uplands currently dominated by western snowberry, the shrub understory is either void of grass or has dense mats of Kentucky bluegrass, a species that thrives in relatively shaded, cool, moist microenvironments particularly under a grazing regime (Kirsch and Kruse 1973; Pelton 1953; Bird 1971; Anderson and Bailey 1979). But as western snowberry stands age, smooth brome invades and within 5-10 years, dominates the site. Under some of these conditions, native grasses and forbs are still present but are significantly suppressed. If brome has begun to invade a site by the time a first prescribed burn is conducted, brome will dominate the site in less than three years. The major vegetation problem swings from dominance by woody plants to dominance by smooth brome.

Refuge croplands include those farmed prior to Refuge establishment in 1935 and not farmed afterwards (about 9 percent of uplands), and those farmed by the Service until the mid-1950's (15 percent of uplands). Croplands farmed prior to 1935 generally were not seeded to perennial cover and were subsequently invaded by a few native grasses and forbs but more commonly exotic grasses and extensive stands of woody plants. Croplands farmed by the Refuge staff, however, were mostly seeded to exotic grasses and alfalfa. These areas, now nearly all dominated by smooth brome, pose substantial threat to the integrity of surrounding native grassland. Such areas need to be restored to native grasses and forbs.

Other conspicuous features of the current landscape are spots of leafy spurge and caragana (see Map 3). In the northern prairie, aspen typically pioneers and spreads along wetland borders (Maini 1960). Leafy spurge, is a very invasive noxious weed in many upland habitats if not controlled (North Dakota Department of Agriculture 1993). First reported and treated on Lostwood in 1958, spurge invaded about 300 acres by 1997, but through control measures, less than a third of that has active growing spurge today. Spurge's typical growth pattern on the Refuge is small dense clones in widely separated spots (280 "spots"), usually about 10-20 yards wide. A higher probability exists of spurge invading in trees than other Refuge habitat types (28 percent of the spurge on 2 percent of the land), and the least probability in native grassland (46 percent of the spurge on 70 percent of the land), and no significant difference than expected on croplands (24 percent of the spurge on 28 percent of the land). Caragana, a tall, nonnative shrub planted by homesteaders at 20 locations on the Refuge, has spread and now occupies about 62 acres and increasing. Stands become so shaded and dense that no other vegetation grows in the understory.

Map 1 Area

Map 2 - Vicinity

Map 3

Areas that were not disturbed by cultivation hold a scattered pattern of Native American "tipi rings," as well as numerous bison "rub rocks." An unexplored wealth of information on how Native Americans used this area lies among these hills and wetlands. More recent human use is evidenced by a couple of intact foundations from old sod houses.

Acquisition

Lostwood Refuge's Executive Order boundary would comprise 33,045 acres. The current Refuge acreage is 26,904 acres, all within the approved boundary. Map 4 shows the Refuge Boundary as established under the 1935 Executive Order 7171; a copy of that Order with the legal descriptions it lists is in Appendix J. Any lands not already acquired as set forth in the Executive Order of September 4, 1935, will be considered individually if presented to the Service for acquisition in the future. In deciding which lands will be accepted for purchase, economic aspects will be included as part of routine planning process. The Service will only acquire lands from willing sellers. Therefore, these lands will remain in private ownership until acquisition opportunities arise.

Environmental Assessment Summary

Preferred Alternative

In the 1994 Environmental Assessment (EA) entitled "Management of upland habitats on Lostwood National Wildlife Refuge," the preferred management alternative of three, was "Enhanced Management." This CCP tiers off of that EA. To attain habitat conditions described in this alternative, will take greater than 15 years, longer than the 15-year span of the CCP. Below is the preferred alternative description, as presented in the EA.

"Selection of this alternative would demand expanded efforts to manage upland habitats on Lostwood Refuge. Upland habitat monitoring and evaluation would be emphasized and management planning would be implemented. Additional facility development on the Refuge would allow increased use of management tools. Managers would be aware of the latest research and literature pertaining to upland management and new methods and practices would be implemented where appropriate. Utility of upland management tools would increase.

Under this alternative, grasslands that have deteriorated in the past would receive intensive management, if needed. Management tools (rest excluded) may be applied in consecutive or alternate years until plant vigor and species diversity in native grasslands improve to acceptable levels. This management strategy is commonly referred to as the restoration phase. When plant vigor and diversity are acceptable, the maintenance phase would be initiated. In this phase, the tool "rest" would be used more frequently. Grasslands may only be actively managed once every 4 or 5 years, resulting in 20-25 percent of Refuge upland area being treated in a given year. Plant vigor and species diversity would not be allowed to deteriorate to the point that necessitates restoration management to meet Refuge goals and objectives.

Diversity and production of indigenous migratory birds and other native wildlife would increase due to improved habitat conditions (Wiens 1970; Kantrud 1981). Height and density of herbaceous vegetation would increase (Vogl 1967). Succession would increase until the upland would be in a dynamic seral stage characteristic of native grasslands (Ryan 1990). Over the long-term, noxious weeds would decrease, and introduced, cool season grasses would decrease in native grasslands. Plant species diversity would increase. Little club moss would be present. The water cycle, mineral cycle, and energy flow would increase (Vogl 1974; Wright and Bailey 1982).

Opportunities for consumptive and non-consumptive recreation would increase. The affect on the local economy would be positive due to increased economic opportunities from grazing and haying. Less noxious weed control would be needed by neighbors. Income derived through local purchases of materials, and income derived indirectly from increased recreational use would increase.

The public image of the Service would improve. The ability of the Service to accomplish goals unrelated to Refuges would improve. Private landowners would be more willing to participate in cooperative wildlife enhancement activities on their lands. Wildlife habitat would improve on private lands also. Neighbors would see the benefits of upland management practices and would likely implement them on their own land. The Service's acquisition program would be viewed with much more favor.

If this alternative were adopted, the purposes and objectives established for Lostwood Refuge would be fully accomplished. Diversity and production of indigenous migratory birds and other native wildlife would increase due to improved habitat conditions. This would also likely occur on private lands because of the circumstances cited above. This alternative is compatible with the purposes for which the Refuge was acquired.

This alternative involves a greater use of a combination of upland management tools to achieve the desired results. Even though the enhanced management alternative is preferred, staff and budget constraints may prevent the full implementation of this alternative. . . ."

Consequences

Without fire, woody plants have spread, including aspen trees, usually surrounding wetlands, changing Lostwood Refuge from a herbaceous grassland to aspen parkland.

The importance of this alternative is unclear until one studies how the whole grassland system functions together. To provide high-quality habitat for maintenance and production of grassland migratory birds and other wildlife, upland vegetation must be in a healthy and vigorous state. This is accomplished through periodic disturbance involving partial or total defoliation of the vegetation, simulating two historical events, short, intensive grazing by native herbivores and wildfires. These defoliation events reduce buildup of residual vegetation, and thus increase energy flow, water, and nutrient cycling (Vogl 1974; Wright and Bailey 1982, Bragg 1995, Bragg and Steuter 1996).

Management of Lostwood Refuge from the 1930's to the late 1970's was based on the best management practices known, focusing on light grazing by livestock through the plant growing season, or leaving areas idle for up to several decades (intentional rest). It is now known, however, such management degrades northern mixed-grass prairie (Kirsch and Kruse 1973, Ryan 1990, Bragg and Steuter 1996). Lack of fire, too much of the same type of grazing, and, in some cases, over-rest have resulted in overwhelming vegetation problems and loss of endemic wildlife.

Currently, unburned areas of the Refuge could be considered aspen parkland (Murphy 1993), and in these areas, the change may soon be irreversible. Grassland and grassland wildlife values on Lostwood Refuge will continue to diminish as documented by Refuge and research staff on these areas. Grassland ecosystems in North America are decreasing in quantity and quality, including that of the Missouri Coteau in the northern Great Plains. A critical need prevails to aggressively act to reverse the trend toward parkland on Lostwood Refuge.

Experimental prescribed burning began on Lostwood Refuge in 1972 with two small areas (less than 20 acres each), when objectives and guidelines were first written for the Refuge, introducing the idea of returning fire to the ecosystem. Prescribed burning was not tried again until 1978. If woody and exotic vegetation are to be reduced, frequent defoliation with fire is needed (Bailey 1988). Refuge uplands require intensive treatment for 10-20 years to get them back into the proper condition after too many years of rest and lack of, or inappropriate, defoliation. In 1978, a more intensive prescribed burning program began. Sixteen percent of the Refuge received several prescribed burns over the next eight years. Simple evaluations were used to review initial wildlife and vegetation responses and trends. When these evaluations (USFWS, unpubl. Refuge files) revealed trends in the desired direction, management expanded, and evaluation efforts were intensified. When results were not desirable, the management approach was revised, and reevaluated again to review trends. From information gathered between 1978-91, the 1972 goals were refined in 1991. This process of prescribing and applying a management technique, evaluating the outcome, then adjusting management as needed, is known as Adaptive Resource Management (ARM). Walters (1986) defines ARM as an "... approach [beginning] with the central tenet that management involves a continual learning process that cannot conveniently be separated into functions like 'research' and [management] ...." He suggests using management as a learning process, as a tool for experimentation. Lostwood Refuge's native prairie resources were rapidly being diminished by succession and alien species, and management began using ARM to reverse the trend. The entire process is one of building blocks, one of continual and improved predictions, evaluations, and changes that over the long-term (20-50 years for Lostwood's prairie) helps accomplish Lostwood Refuge's mission, goals, and objectives. Another of these building blocks is the 1998 CCP that more explicitly defines Lostwood Refuge's mission, goals, and objectives. Setting clear, quantified objectives, helps focus long-term management, which is essential to successful natural resource conservation.

Map 4

A dynamic ecological event took place in 1988 that likely demonstrates fire's role in preventing the establishment of trees and other woody plants. That year, prairie soils and vegetation were as dry as they have been since perhaps the drought years of the mid-1930's. Lightning struck and ignited fire on the Lostwood Wilderness Area in August, after no rain had fallen for a month, wetlands had been dry for two years, and strong hot winds (30-40 mph) had prevailed throughout summer. Healthy aspen trees, from saplings to mature trees (1.5 feet dbh and larger), had little moisture in their trunks. The wildfire burned through large aspen trees at ground level, and those not burned through were heat-girdled (fire destroyed the cambium layer in the lower trunk). Where shrubs occurred, fire burned deep into the roots and humus. Where only grasses and forbs occurred, however, fire swept across without burning beyond root crowns and humus (USFWS, unpubl. Refuge files). Likewise, areas dominated by grasses "greened up" in September, but areas previously dominated by woody plants remained black with exposed mineral soils and no new growth. This fire suggests some historical mechanisms by which woody plants were suppressed and grasses were favored in prairie.

By fall 1997, 65 percent of Refuge uplands had been treated with at least one prescribed burn. Prior to 1993, this program was accomplished with volunteer and few trained, paid professionals. All prescribed burns were controlled safely within planned burn boundaries. During 1993-1997, additional staff were hired and trained specifically for the fire program, and fire equipment and facilities were improved. If this type of funding and staffing continues, the prescribed burning program will progress, except for evaluations. Funds and staff are insufficient for proper evaluation and monitoring however. In addition to fire, prairies evolved with a significant grazing influence. From about 1940-1982, Refuge grazing treatments did not simulate historical grazing intensity and duration (large bison herds grazing an area heavily in a few days). Grazing, without fire, tends to increase Kentucky bluegrass, western snowberry, and aspen, as previously described. Burning without grazing will limit basal growth potential of native grasses, leaving bare ground exposed for alien species to invade, and apparently does little to reduce competitive ability of smooth brome. By fall 1997, 26 percent of Refuge uplands had been treated with at least one three-year 14-day rotation grazing using livestock. Of this, 9 percent of the uplands had received prescribed burns that reduced the woody plants. Unfortunately, the grazing program is somewhat limited as a tool, due to lack of staff for proper planning, coordinating, monitoring of grazing, and plant and wildlife evaluations.

Croplands dominated by smooth brome, Kentucky bluegrass, quack grass, crested wheatgrass, and snowberry need to be restored to native grasses and forbs. This will reduce the potential for exotic species invasion into native grassland, and will improve habitat for endemic wildlife. Methods to accomplish this task are continually being adopted under the ARM philosophy. Native forb and grass seed best suited for Lostwood Refuge will be purchased, and some will be harvested on-site. Once seeded, frequent defoliation is essential to develop plant root systems so the seeded native plants can function together as a grassland and develop with management. This program lacks funds for staffing, preparing seedbeds, purchasing and harvesting seed, and initial intensive management.

Harvesting of upland hay is another tool for managing upland and wetland habitats on Lostwood Refuge. It is a nonselective (cuts everything at the same time) treatment that stimulates the Fast Nutrient cycle if applied at appropriate times. It also removes excess litter. It is a particularly important tool in managing newly planted herbaceous native plants on croplands. It helps to develop plant root systems, yet leaves behind stubble that protects young plants from severe climatic events. Funds for proper planning and evaluations are lacking.

Integrated Pest Management has been used to control leafy spurge. If not controlled, it will gradually dominate many upland sites, an unfortunate common occurrence across parts of North Dakota and surrounding states. Chemical applications, mechanical treatments (mowing), and prescribed burning have contained spurge on about 60-100 acres of 300 acres infested. Biological control was started in 1995 when leafy spurge beetles (host specific) became available in sufficient quantities at North Dakota nursery sites. As beetles on Lostwood become established and are transported to new spots, chemical dependency will be eliminated except where there are too few plants to support beetles. This program lacks funds to purchase chemicals and to hire personnel for sufficient treatments and evaluations.

Proposed public use, wetland habitat management, cultural resources, and research activities are presented in the Refuge Goals and Objectives section.

Defoliation and Rest--Importance and Methods, and Effects to Habitat and Wildlife

Not defoliating vegetation for one or more years is defined as rest, another management tool. Some units of the Refuge have not been or are rarely managed because of various constraints. Rested habitat is important for many species of migratory and resident birds and other wildlife for reproduction, foraging, and roosting or escape cover. Resting much more than five years, however, is detrimental to the native herbaceous plant community. Some native wildlife species also find too much rest unattractive, as previously discussed. Periodic defoliation treatments are needed to maintain native grasslands in their best ecological condition, and provide appropriate habitat diversity for grassland wildlife.

Native prairie plants have evolved mechanisms that allow them to survive and flourish with periodic flood, drought, grazing, and fire (Ellison 1960; Stubbendieck 1988, Bragg 1995, Bragg and Steuter 1996). One of these adaptations is "mutualism," a type of symbiosis where species coexist to the benefit of each other. Here, the relationship is between a plant and a group of fungi called mycorrhizal fungi (Stoddart *et al.* 1975). About 85-90 percent of all native plants have developed this relationship. Fungi grow in a narrow area along the edge of the roots called the rhizosphere. This zone extends the root system of native plants, increasing a plant's ability to absorb more moisture and nutrients than plants without mycorrhizal fungi. The rhizosphere area is rich with soil microbes that break down soil and old plant material into forms that plants can use for growth (Barbour *et al.* 1980).

Periodic grazing and fire stimulate activity in the rhizosphere and surrounding soil area, thereby fertilizing the plants (Wallace 1987; Bentivenga and Hetrick 1992). Plants without mycorrhiza cannot grow as well, especially when grazed and burned. The whole system is not fully understood, but it is known that two nutrient cycles exist: a "Fast Nutrient cycle" is stimulated by grazing and haying, and a "Slow Nutrient cycle" is accelerated by fire.

Fire: Fire, whether set by humans or caused by lightning, has been a natural part of the prairie for thousands of years (Sauer 1950; Higgins 1986, Bragg 1995, Bragg and Steuter 1996). Fire causes the Slow Nutrient cycle to release nutrients otherwise unavailable to growing plants. Litter (dead plant material from previous years' plant growth) contains nitrogen unavailable for plants until the plant and litter is completely decomposed (Bragg 1995). Accumulation of litter over several years significantly reduces the amount of available nitrogen for plants. Fire breaks down this litter, causing a flurry of microbial activity that releases more nitrogen for plant uptake than would been available without fire (Barbour *et al.* 1980, Wright and Bailey 1982). This increase in microbial activity occurs for up to three years after a fire. Native plants in the northern Great Plains depend on fire to keep nutrient cycles functioning normally.

Heavy layers of litter and excessive humus creates a micro environment that is attractive to exotic grass species (Ode *et al.* 1980). Fire removes litter and reduces humus, producing a more arid soil environment (Bragg and Steuter 1996), a condition unattractive to these exotic species but attractive to most native herbaceous species (Bragg 1995). Removing excessive litter with a prescribed burn under predetermined conditions, decreases the risk of destructive wildfires (Bailey 1988). Fire prevents grasslands from succeeding to shrubland (Sauer 1950). It can also reduce dominance of mosses (Bragg 1995), a desired fire effect on club moss, an allopathic (prevents other plants from establishing) species in the northern Great Plains. Fire can maintain or change a physical vegetation structure to provide desired habitat for indigenous wildlife (Bailey 1988). Fire usually increases species diversity (Anderson and Bailey 1980, Bragg and Steuter 1996), including wetlands (Bailey 1988). Fire produces conditions for native seedling establishment for long-term plant diversity, particularly forbs (Bragg and Steuter 1996).

Nutrient cycles are triggered with fire, and plants respond by producing rich, succulent growth, as shown here in a xeric hill site in late July after a mid-May burn.

Use of fire as a management tool began in 1965 (Higgins *et al.* 1989) in the northern Great Plains. Grasslands are burned primarily to manipulate vegetation, soil microbes, nutrient cycles, and to enhance the biological productivity and diversity of specific organisms, or to accomplish specific objectives (reduce Kentucky bluegrass). Specific objectives may be broad (prairie restoration and maintenance) or narrow (management for endangered or rare species or reduction of a woody plant species), but will contain two characteristics: it is measurable and specifies what specifically will be done. Where native prairie is not a major component of the management area, nearly all prescribed fires are used to: reduce vegetative litter, control noxious weeds, reestablish native grasses through reseeding, or improve the chemical kill on exotic plants prior to reseeding native grasses and forbs. Where native prairie is a major part of a management area, the primary reasons for burning are to restore, improve, or enhance the prairie habitat for wildlife.

Management needed on Lostwood Refuge to return indigenous plant and wildlife species involves three phases. **(1) Renovation**; burning 3-5 times over 7-10 years. Currently 50 percent of Lostwood Refuge is in this phase. **(2) Renovation-maintenance**; in a 7-year period, graze 3 years, rest 2-3 years, and burn 1-2 times. Currently 15 percent of the Refuge is in this phase. **(3) Maintenance**; alternately burn and graze with 2-5 year rest periods. Currently none of the Refuge is in the maintenance phase. From 1978-97, an average of 3.8 burns and 2,410 acres per year were prescribe burned (includes 2 wildfires in 1988 totaling 6,135 acres). From 1990-1997, an average of 3.5 burns and 3,160 acres per year were prescribed burned. Prescribed burns 500 acres or larger usually begin at 1100 hr and end at 1700 hr, resulting in 6 hours per burn day when smoke is emitted. This calculates about 23 hours each year smoke is emitted, or about 0.3 percent of the hours in a year. Cool-season grasses, per pound burned, emitted less than wood burning stoves (Bragg 1995). Grasses, even tall, warm-season grasses, produce far less than trees (Bragg 1995). Water erosion following a prescribed burn in northern mixed-grass prairies was found to be negligible (Bragg 1995). Annual prescribed burn plans are completed and approved, following standard procedures of the U.S. Fish and Wildlife Service.

Fire affects wildlife mainly by modifying habitat (Wright and Bailey 1982, Higgins et al. 1989). Fire reduces vegetative biomass and litter and therefore favors early over later successional stages (Barbour et al. 1980). Succession following a fire defoliation event produces a series of successional changes for different wildlife species. For example, the year of a burn and into the second year provides habitat conditions attractive to lark buntings, chestnut-collared longspurs, and horned larks. The second and third years provide increased vertical cover but open understory that provides preferred habitat for Baird's and grasshopper sparrows. As more litter accumulates in the third and fourth years, Sprague's pipits increase along with nesting cover for waterfowl and resident bird species. In Saskatchewan, Maher (1973) found one of the highest breeding bird densities recorded in any treatment during his study (burn, grazed, un-grazed) on burned grassland during the second year following the burn. Burns also increase local habitat diversity by creating a mosaic of habitats and increasing habitat interspersion and edge (Biondini *et al.* 1989; Steuter *et al.* 1990). Some direct mortality of wildlife can result from fire (Wright and Bailey 1982, Higgins *et al.* 1989). Most often this occurs in sedentary species such as some reptiles or immobile life stages, as in the egg or pupal stage of many insects. Although fire can be detrimental to some ground nesting birds, prescribed burns may be timed to avoid overlap with nesting seasons. Some prescribed burns may have to be done during the nesting season to impact plant species to be encouraged or discouraged. Many species of birds, however, are known to successfully re-nest following such disturbances or initiate nests in recently burned prairie (Kirsch and Kruse 1973; Kruse and Piehl 1986).

Grazing: Grazing stimulates the Fast Nutrient cycle only during a portion of a plant's growth period called the "window period" (based on plant physiological responses [Manske 1994, 1996], about June 1 to July 15 for cool-season grasses and about June 15 to July 31 for warm-season grasses in northwestern North Dakota). To understand this, a little further explanation may be helpful. About 85 percent of nitrogen in prairie soil is tied up as organic nitrogen, a nitrogen form not available for plant growth. When mycorrhizal fungi-dependent plants are grazed during the window period, microbial activity helps convert organic nitrogen to mineral nitrogen. When aptly grazed, the plant's nitrogen is removed (primarily in the aboveground leaves) and the plant releases carbon in the form of simple sugar released into the rhizosphere (Coyne et al. 1995). This causes an increase in bacteria activity that in turn causes protozoa and nematodes (soil microbes) to also increase activity. They give off ammonia. Mycorrhizal fungi absorb the ammonia and convert it to nitrate, which is a mineral form of nitrogen, usable by plants. Nitrogen is passed from the fungi to the plant. The defoliated plant has been stimulated to activate axillary buds (new leaves that can tiller the year grazed) and the nitrogen from the rhizosphere provides the nutrients. This increases plant growth (Barbour *et al.* 1980, Manske 1996). Native plants in the northern Great Plains depend on grazing to retain a normal nutrient cycle.

Plants can easily be overgrazed (i.e., repeated defoliation of individual plants over weeks or months) during window periods. Indeed, grasslands grow most vigorously with short periods of grazing during the window period. Historically, bison probably did not stay and repeatedly graze a given area for very long (Larson 1940; Edwards 1978). Grazing should not exceed 14 days at the recommended rate of 2-3 acres/AUM (Animal Unit Month) for this area (U.S. Soil Conservation Service 1975).

Primary components of grazing are timing and intensity (Stoddart *et al.* 1975). Timing refers to the time of year and length of time the plants are exposed to grazing animals (grazing period), including the number of grazing periods. Intensity refers to the degree of grazing pressure that plants and plant communities experience. Intensity is a function of stocking density and grazing period length, and is controlled by the number of livestock in a given area (stocking rate) and is measured in AUMs (Animal Unit Months)/acre. These factors are managed to achieve a controlled grazing program. For the purposes of management on Lostwood Refuge, grazing and animal impact will be considered one tool; both are means of removing herbage, i.e., defoliation. While we recognize the difference between the two, one cannot be used without the other (See Appendix B, Glossary of Terms for definition of grazing and animal impact.)

Grassland is the dominant upland habitat on Lostwood Refuge. Native grasses and most native forbs in the northern Great Plains evolved with and require periodic partial or total defoliation followed by periods of rest to maintain their vigor and preserve floral richness (reviewed above). Vegetative vigor and diversity are paramount to achieve the landscape description for the Refuge. Grazing is one of the primary tools available to accomplish the goals and objectives, relying on livestock provided by local livestock producers. A critical part of a successful grazing program is informing cooperating livestock producers of the goals and objectives of the Refuge, and how their efforts contribute to successful Refuge management.

Grazing on Lostwood Refuge will not be restricted to warm or cool season growth periods. Grazing may take place during slow and fast growth stages and during the dormant period, depending on the specific habitat objective. In most cases, grazing is intended to stimulate the Fast Nutrient cycle that promotes growth (Coleman *et al.* 1983). The period of time the plants and plant communities are exposed to livestock will vary, though will be minimized as much as possible. Usually the grazing period will not exceed 14 consecutive days (Manske 1994). Stocking rates will vary depending on specific objectives.

Grazing affects grasslands and wildlife. Effects can be good or bad, depending on the type of grazing and how it is used. If used correctly in upland areas, grazing will improve wildlife habitat for many species. Effects of grazing on grasslands and wildlife have been heavily researched, yet many questions remain unanswered. On Lostwood Refuge, spring grazing reduced densities of mallards, gadwalls, and blue-winged teal (Kruse and Bowen, 1996); nest density of gadwalls increased after grazing ended. Nest success, however, was uninfluenced by grazing. Sedivec *et al.* (1990) concluded that cattle grazing enhanced waterfowl nesting habitat in south-central North Dakota when properly managed by specialized grazing systems. Moderately grazed grasslands in Iowa were more attractive to blue-winged teal than un-grazed habitats (Burgess *et al.* 1965). Many other studies have found grazing detrimental to duck production (Kirsch 1969; Miller 1971; Gjersing 1975; Mundinger 1976; Kirsch *et al.* 1978). In central Montana, the greatest density of duck pairs occurred on grasslands that were un-grazed during the previous year (Mundinger 1976). Results of studies are often confusing and conflicting, due to different habitats, wildlife, and grazing types used among studies (Kirsch *et al.* 1978, Kirby *et al.* 1992).

Research on effects of grazing on other migratory birds in the Prairie Pothole Region is less plentiful. Grazing mainly affects habitats of rangeland birds by reducing vegetation quantity and quality (Kirsch *et al.* 1978, Strassman 1987). Specific effects of grazing on breeding birds, however, are not uniform or easily defined because of differences in grazing intensity and rangeland type. Owens and Myres (1973), Kantrud (1981), and Messmer (1985) found that grazing reduced or eliminated some nongame birds, while not affecting or increasing populations of others; some species preferred grazed over idle grasslands. Total bird density in North Dakota prairies generally increases with increased grazing intensity (Kantrud and Kologiski 1983), although species richness generally decreases (Kantrud 1981; Kantrud and Kologiski 1983). Upland nesting shorebirds such as marbled godwit and willet prefer prairie of short vegetation, such as that disturbed by grazing (Ryan *et al.* 1984; Ryan and Renken 1987). Upland sandpipers, however, might not initiate nests when cattle are present in mixed-grass prairie (Bowen and Kruse 1993), and prefer lightly grazed or idle areas (Higgins *et al.* 1969). Nest sites, foraging habitats, or prey of several species of raptors at Lostwood Refuge, especially ferruginous hawks and burrowing owls, have been negatively affected by increases in vegetation height and density under decades of light grazing or rest (Murphy 1993). Ferruginous hawks and burrowing owls seem to prefer heavily grazed tracts in the northern Plains (Schmutz *et al.* 1980; Konrad and Gilmer 1984; Haug and Oliphant 1990). Kirsch *et al.* (1978) concluded that annual grazing reduces production of most upland nesting birds, although periodic treatments are needed to maintain upland nesting habitats in their best ecological condition. Effects of grazing on bird populations, positive or negative, are greatly complicated by variation in climate, topography, and soils across the northern Great Plains (Kantrud and Kologiski 1983).

Rest: Rest can also be an important management tool. The northern mixed-grass prairies historically were not grazed season-long, or even parts of a year, year-after-year. Some grassland wildlife species require freshly burned areas during part of their lives, some require grazed areas, and some need areas rested for several years, providing accumulations of litter for nesting cover (Kantrud 1981; Ryan 1990). Litter is also important to building topsoil. However, rest for more than five years decreases "beneficial" microbes in the soils that stimulate Fast and Slow Nutrient cycles (Coleman *et al.* 1983). In addition, woody plants increase in areas only grazed or rested, ultimately decreasing native grasses and forbs (Bragg and Steuter 1996). In summary, litter builds topsoils, but too much litter over too long of a period ties up much of the nutrients. Fire, which historically occurred at least every 5-10 years (reviewed above), helps circulate these nutrients and maintain the grass/forb composition.

For the purpose of upland management on Lostwood Refuge, rest is defined as intentionally allowing upland habitat to remain undisturbed for one year or longer. Some units of the Refuge have not been or are rarely managed because of various constraints. This unintentional lack of disturbance is not considered "rest." Rest will be used as a tool to meet objectives established for the Refuge.

Past management of Lostwood Refuge followed contemporary philosophies and practices thought to be best for wildlife. With increased knowledge, however, management became more fine-tuned and techniques have improved. Native wildlife in the northern Great Plains need mosaics of grassland habitats to maintain their diversity and abundance (Ryan 1990). Without one or more of the historical treatments, the plant diversity regresses and abundance of native grassland wildlife suffers. Disturbances must be relatively short in duration and vary from partial to total defoliation to maintain natural patch dynamics (Hulbert 1969; Huber and Steuter 1984; Bragg 1995). These disturbances also provide varied vegetation height and density, successional stages, and amounts of residual cover required by migratory birds (Madden 1996).

The importance of undisturbed cover for upland nesting waterfowl is well documented (Keith 1961; Burgess *et al.* 1965; Duebbert 1969; Oetting and Cassel 1971; Page and Cassel 1971; Duebbert and Kantrud 1974; Kirsch *et al.* 1978; Kaiser *et al.* 1979; Voorhees and Cassel 1980). Research also indicates that long periods of rest may reduce the attractiveness of cover to nesting waterfowl (Voorhees and Cassel 1980, Higgins and Barker 1982, Kemner 1989).

Importance of undisturbed cover for other migratory birds varies among species. Passerine breeding densities in North Dakota may be lower in undisturbed prairie than in grazed and hayed areas, but species richness may follow the opposite pattern (Kantrud 1981). Baird's sparrows, which nest at relatively high densities at Lostwood Refuge, need mainly grass-forb, native prairie vegetation of moderate height and density (Sousa and McDonal 1983), such as that produced after a year of rest from haying or burning. Northern harriers and short-eared owls nest mainly in undisturbed grasslands or lightly grazed grasslands (Toland 1986; Kantrud and Higgins 1992), but ferruginous hawks, Swainson's hawks, and burrowing owls need closely grazed prairies for foraging or nesting (Wakeley 1978; Kantrud 1981; Jasikoff 1982; Kantrud and Kologiski 1983; Sharp 1986; Haug and Oliphant 1990). Kirsch *et al.* (1978) concluded that annual cover removal is detrimental to the production of most upland nesting birds but acknowledged that periodic treatment is needed. As reviewed elsewhere in this document, periodic treatments are desired to maintain native, upland nesting habitats in their best ecological condition. Therefore, long periods of rest are detrimental.

Rest will be used at Lostwood Refuge in a manner that takes full advantage of its beneficial effects and minimizes potential detrimental effects. Primary components of rest are timing and duration. Rest will be used to provide residual standing vegetation during fall, winter, and spring for use by upland nesting waterfowl, other migratory birds, and other wildlife as resting, roosting, bedding, feeding, fawning, nesting, and escape cover. Rest will not be overused in order to keep succession, water and mineral cycles, energy flow, and quality of cover at high levels in native prairie. The length of rest will depend on the condition of the grassland. Those in poor condition may not improve with rest unless other management tools are used to improve condition prior to rest. Native grasslands in very good condition can benefit for the first two to three years and may sustain several more years of rest before deteriorating significantly. Due to the invasion of exotic, cool season grasses in native grasslands on Lostwood Refuge, habitat conditions quickly deteriorate if over-rested. Conditions may deteriorate to the point that intensive management is needed for recovery. Appropriate use of rest ensures long-term health of native grasslands, requiring less intensive use of other tools.

Haying: Haying stimulates the Fast Nutrient cycle if applied during the window period, but in contrast to grazing it is nonselective (haying cuts everything uniformly while livestock graze selectively). The use of haying as a grassland management tool on the Lostwood Refuge relies on local livestock producers. No upland management program using haying as a tool will be successful if it does not meet needs of these producers, i.e., grass cut too late for nutritional value. However, haying activities will be complete by September 1 to allow regrowth for winter cover and residual cover needed by ground-nesting birds the following spring. Other haying activities such as baling and removal of bales will also be accomplished by September 1. Haying will not normally be conducted more than once per year on a given area. In most cases, haying will not be done annually, but only periodically (every 4-7 years) to maintain grassland vigor.

Studies of waterfowl production in tame grass plantings have shown that nesting ducks prefer un-mowed over mowed upland vegetation (Oetting and Cassel 1971; Duebbert and Kantrud 1974; Kirsch *et al.* 1978; Voorhees and Cassel 1980). This can be attributed to needs for residual vegetation especially by early nesting ducks (Gates 1965; Martz 1967; Luttschwager and Higgins 1991). Although ducks prefer un-mowed vegetation, they can have relatively good production in early successional growth the first year after haying (Oetting and Cassel 1971; Vorhees and Cassel 1980; Luttschwager and Higgins 1991). Periodic haying of seeded nesting cover has also been shown to be an effective means of managing grassland to enhance duck production (Kemner 1989). Higgins and Barker (1982) found that seeded nesting cover reached peak growth in 3 to 5 years, and renovation was needed to maintain stand height-density and vitality. Timing of haying is critical; haying during nesting can cause up to 100 percent destruction of active nests (Labisky 1957).

Research on effects of haying on other migratory birds and other grassland-dependent wildlife is more limited. Higgins *et al.* (1969) found that intermittently mowed cover was excellent nesting habitat for upland plovers. Annual haying has been implicated as a major cause of population declines of the bobolink (Bollinger *et al.* 1990). Kirsch *et al.* (1978) concluded that annual haying is detrimental to the production of most upland nesting birds, although periodic treatments may be needed to maintain upland nesting habitats in their best ecological condition. Mowing of grasslands has been recommended as a management tool for willets and marbled godwits in the northern Great Plains (Ryan *et al.* 1984; Ryan and Renken 1987). Early haying of meadows in Europe has markedly altered nesting chronology and species composition of nesting migratory birds (Beintema *et al.* 1985; Pfeifer and Brandl 1991). Among small rodents common to the northern Great Plains, haying generally causes declines in abundance of meadow voles but increased abundance of deer mice (Eadie 1953; LoBue and Darnell 1959; Lemen and Clausen 1984; McGowan and Bookhout 1986; Kotler *et al.* 1988).

As reviewed above, the whole grassland system was kept active and healthy by periodic grazing, fire impact, and rest; without these treatments, native plants decline and changes in the plant community occur. Without these three treatments, nonnative plants to the Lostwood area such as smooth brome, Kentucky bluegrass, quack grass, and leafy spurge, were competitively favored and increased. Returning fire and simulating bison using livestock in shorter durations will return indigenous flora and fauna but will take 10-20 years of intensive management to see the long-term results.

Twelve different species of waterfowl nest on Lostwood Refuge.

The following habitat conditions describe the landscape that will best meet the needs of native, breeding migratory birds and will help achieve goals and objectives of the Refuge.

Succession: A mosaic of native prairie communities will be present with a predominance of habitats in seral, mid-successional stages that approach a pristine condition (i.e., Ryan 1990). Grasses and forbs will be mainly perennial species native to northern mixed-grass prairie. Composition of grasses will vary depending on soil type and location on slopes, which affect soil moisture regimes. Plants will be of mixed ages. Western snowberry will be maintained at less than 25 percent canopy coverage. The goal is to have no more than 300 aspen clumps with an average size of no more than 0.5 acres/clump. Uplands previously farmed and now dominated by smooth brome, quack grass, or Kentucky bluegrass will be reseeded to native grasses and forbs, except perhaps the Lostwood Wilderness Area where vehicle access is, for the most part (i.e., emergencies), prohibited.

Water Cycle: In general, soils and soil surfaces will be permeable, well aerated, and covered with plant litter in most years. Soil organic content will also be high. Water runoff from rain events will be low due to litter and well established root systems in the soil (Bragg 1995). Even in the year of a prescribed burn, slight, if any, reduction in infiltration and percolation rates will occur, persisting for only one or two years (Bragg 1995).

Mineral Cycle: An active mineral cycle will exist with minimal runoff or erosion from precipitation. Surface litter will decompose, preventing buildup of old matted dead vegetation, yet preserving a surface mulch. Moderate to substantial amounts of residual standing vegetation will be present during the winter and early growing season on most of the Refuge. Other areas recently burned provide relatively snow-free areas for winter feeding. This provides critical winter cover and feeding habitat for resident wildlife and also residual and open nesting habitat for the various grassland birds the following spring. The healthy grass, forb, and shrub component will promote deeper recycling of minerals from subsurface to surface. Shallow-rooted, introduced species, such as Kentucky bluegrass, will be discouraged in native sod by increasing the competitive ability of desirable species. This will prevent litter buildup, hasten low mineral cycling, improve height-density of residual vegetation, and improve vegetative species diversity. High insect and microorganism activity will exist at and below the soil surface.

Energy Flow: A moderately high energy flow will be present as indicated by the high density of plants on the ground surface through periodic defoliation from fire and grazing events. A variety of both warm and cool season grass and forb species will be present in the native grasslands, resulting in a longer season of plant growth, increased solar energy harvest, and more upright, residual cover during periods of rest.

REFUGE GOALS AND OBJECTIVES

Lostwood Refuge is the only large block of federally-owned land in the pothole region of the northern Great Plain's mixed-grass prairie. It has a rich mix of prairie and wetland resources found nowhere else in the Refuge System. The decision to purchase this unique and diverse area was based on two Federal biologist's observations recorded in the mid-1910's. It is from these early recordings that the following mission was established for Lostwood Refuge.

Mission

"To restore and preserve the indigenous biological communities of the mid- to late-1800's on a representative sample of the physiographic region known as the Missouri Coteau of the northern Great Plains' mixed-grass prairie."

To meet this mission, management must be flexible, changing and adapting with information obtained through monitoring and research. It is essential to apply Adaptive Resource Management to Lostwood Refuge, and recognize management as a continual learning process with variation and change as essential ingredients. If Lostwood Refuge is to progress and meet the goals and objectives, then management activity tools must be viewed as experimental. Research and management must work as a team towards meeting these goals and objectives.

Lostwood Refuge's vista should embrace the native plant and wildlife community. It should represent a simulation of what was first observed here at the turn of the 19th century. It should be a wavy sea of native warm and cool season grasses sprinkled with colorful floral displays throughout the growing seasons. It should abound in indigenous grassland and wetland birds and other wildlife including sparrows, ducks, shorebirds, geese, longspurs, grebes, pipits, grouse, deer, hawks, and much more. It should be a place for people to enjoy through wildlife-dependent recreational opportunities, including hunting, wildlife observation and photography, and environmental education and interpretation. Herein we present Lostwood Refuge's goals, objectives for each goal, and strategies on how to obtain each objective.

Goals, Objectives, and Strategies

Presented below are Lostwood Refuge's seven goals and respective objectives. Accompanying each objective are associated strategies, which are ongoing and adaptive.

1) Endangered Species Goal: *To preserve, restore, and enhance indigenous flora and fauna that are candidate, threatened, endangered, or species of special interest.*

Objective A. Maintain at least 9 breeding pairs of piping plovers and increase, where possible, habitat to accommodate at least 16 additional breeding pairs, with a mean fledging rate at least 1.2 young per breeding pair (Ryan *et al.* 1993).

Strategies:

- Monitor reproductive success of pairs through fledging to evaluate effects of management activities on piping plovers.

- Maintain and improve shoreline habitat (i.e., prescribed burning, grazing, salt applications, gravel addition).

- Protect beaches and nests from predators (i.e., by use of barrier fences).

- Create new nesting beaches where appropriate.

Objective B. Provide protection and habitat for the following migrant threatened and endangered species: peregrine falcon, bald eagle, and whooping crane.

Strategies:

- Provide attractive shoreline habitats for shorebirds, a staple prey for migrating peregrine falcons.

- Provide roosting sites during the fall for migrating snow geese, a staple prey for migrating bald eagles.

- Provide exposed shorelines and grazed or burned uplands for spring and fall migrating whooping cranes.

Objective C. Maintain and increase breeding populations of endemic species and other unique northern mixed-grass species that are declining throughout much of their range due to habitat loss, such as Baird's sparrow, Sprague's pipit, marbled godwit, ferruginous hawk, mealy primrose, and Dakota skipper.

Strategies:

■ Monitor vegetation management to evaluate effects on endemic species and other indigenous fauna.

■ Provide a mix of plant successional stages, using management tools such as fire, grazing, and rest to maximize native biodiversity.

Objective D. Consider reintroduction of greater sandhill crane, trumpeter swan, and western burrowing owl.

Strategies:

■ Assess the potential of reintroducing these species.

2) Other Wildlife Goal: *To develop and maintain diversity and abundance of fauna indigenous to the northern Missouri Coteau.*

Objective A. Achieve an average annual duck production of 14,000 (striving for an average of 7,500 breeding pairs and Mayfield hatching success of at least 25 percent) and an average of 70 giant Canada goose pairs.

Strategies:

■ Monitor duck and goose breeding population size and duck reproductive success to evaluate effects of management activities.

■ Monitor coyote, fox, raccoon, skunk, and badger populations to assess potential predation risk of local ground-nesting birds.

■ Maintain whole or part of 4 to 6 coyote territories on the Refuge to keep red fox to less than or equal to 3 breeding territories; higher duck hatching success has been shown in coyote versus fox territories (Sovada *et al.* 1995).

■ Keep raccoon numbers to less than 6 individuals on the Refuge by reducing den sites (i.e., hollow trees, rock piles, old buildings adjacent to boundary), or removal of an individual, as a last resort (raccoons are a major predator on ducks [Johnson *et al.* 1989]).

■ Produce habitat attractive to grassland dependent raptors but not to red-tailed hawks and great-horned owls, by minimizing the number and size of tree clumps as described in the Wildland Goal, Objective B, through periodic prescribed burning and grazing.

■ Provide interspersed blocks of rested nesting cover for upland nesting ducks.

■ Provide, where possible, emergent cover for over-water nesting ducks.

Objective B. Achieve an average number of occupied nesting areas for ferruginous hawk of 3 to 5, for Swainson's hawk 5 to 10 with both of their productivity greater than 1.6 young per occupied territory; for red-tailed hawk less than 13, and for great-horned owl less than 10.

Strategies:

■ Monitor raptor nesting density and productivity to evaluate the effects of management.

■ Consider nesting platforms for ferruginous hawks where Refuge lands adjoin privately-owned native pastures that support abundant Richardson's ground squirrels and meet the hawk's other biological needs.

■ Provide grassland habitat attractive to ferruginous and Swainson's hawks and minimize competition from red-tailed hawks and great-horned owls by reducing the number and size of tree clumps as described in Wildland Goal, Objective B.

Objective C. Achieve an average, annual breeding densities (singing males/100 acres [based on point-counts in an 82-yard radius]) for the following passerines: chestnut-colored longspur, western meadowlark, Sprague's pipit, and Le Conte's sparrow greater than 1 male; Baird's sparrow and grasshopper sparrow greater than 8 males; savannah sparrow greater than 10 males; clay-colored sparrow from 4 to 15 males; and common yellowthroat from 1 to 5 males.

Strategies:

■ Monitor breeding passerine species abundance and reproductive success.

■ Provide different plant successional stages using management tools, such as fire, grazing, and rest, that will maximize indigenous biodiversity and abundance.

Objective D. Achieve minimum densities (pairs/100 acres) of 1 upland sandpiper, 1 marbled godwit, 1 willet, and 2 Wilson's phalarope (in areas with appropriate adjacent wetlands) over a 5-year period average.

Strategies:

■ Monitor abundance of upland-nesting shorebirds.

■ Provide different plant successional stages using management tools such as fire, grazing and rest, that will maximize shorebird biodiversity and abundance.

Objective E. Achieve over a 5-year period an average spring sharp-tailed grouse population (males attending leks) of at least 600 males.

Strategies:

■ Monitor spring grouse populations and nesting.

■ Provide different plant successional stages using management tools such as fire, grazing, and rest, that will maximize abundance.

Objective F. Maintain diversity of other indigenous vertebrate and invertebrate species in balance with other goals and objectives of Lostwood Refuge.

Strategies:

■ Establish a biological monitoring program using a species or a group of species that can represent other species for each habitat type.

■ Inventory invertebrates in soils, wetlands, and plants in different habitat types and successional stages.

■ Develop, after inventories, strategies to effectively maintain and increase indigenous species of concern.

■ Plan management that incorporates the needs of native communities for each management unit, and accomplish Refuge management through an ecosystem approach.

Objective G. Private lands within the original approved boundary may be purchased from willing sellers to provide additional habitat for migratory birds and other wildlife.

Strategies:

■ Provide an easy step for landowners to use when interested in selling their land for inclusion into Lostwood Refuge.

3) Wildlands Goal: *To restore and maintain native plant communities that occurred in the late 1800's (prior to homesteading by people of European descent) in an ecological relationship with vertebrates and invertebrates.*

Objective A. Manage upland native flora to sustain the following dominant associations, **moist or mesic sites** porcupine grass, big bluestem, tufted hairgrass, prairie dropseed, mat muhly, prairie cordgrass, blazing star, prairie lily, two-grooved milkvetch; **slopes or moderate moisture sites** with species such as green needlegrass, western wheatgrass, prairie sandreed, rough fescue, narrow-leafed poisonvetch, blanketflower, purple prairie clover; **dry or xeric sites** with species such as blue grama, bluebunch wheatgrass, plains muhly, spike oat, Sandberg bluegrass, early bluegrass, needle-and-thread, spotted gayfeather, purple coneflower, golden aster (for list of scientific names, see Appendix K).

Strategies:

■ Prescribe burn areas under **renovation phase** 3 to 5 times with 1 to 2 years rest between each burn; prescribe burn **renovation-maintenance phase** at least twice and graze at least 3 years in a 10-year period; and prescribe burn **maintenance phase** at least once every 6 years and graze 3 years out of 10 with less than 6 years rest between treatments.

■ Identify plant community types that represent indigenous flora in soil types and topography using the Federal Vegetation Classification and Information Standards (Federal Geographic Data Committee, Vegetation Subcommittee 1996).

■ Develop techniques to monitor effects of management practices on vegetation structure and litter depth.

■ Determine what soil nutrient cycles, soil invertebrates and other living soil organisms are needed, and how to maintain these conditions, for native flora.

■ Stimulate the Fast Nutrient cycle by grazing in a short-duration rotation.

■ Prescribe-burn during different burning periods to attain specific objectives (i.e., reducing smooth brome when at the 3-6 leaf stage, reducing woody plants during mid-July to late August).

■ When native grasses and forbs comprise less than 50 percent canopy cover, reseed old fields to native herbaceous varieties suited to this area and Refuge-harvested seed, and monitor wildlife and plant responses.

Objective B. Maintain western snowberry and snowberry/silverberry at less than 25 percent canopy coverage, and trees at less than or equal to 300 clumps of quacking aspen with an average size 0.5 acres/clump.

Strategies:

■ Prescribe burn to reduce small shrubs to reach the fauna objectives.

■ Prescribe burn and use of other tools (i.e., chemical injections) for obtaining the aspen objective that accomplishes the fauna objectives.

■ Use grazing to encourage indigenous grasses and forbs that will reduce woody plants.

Objective C. Attempt to eradicate exotic species or at least reduce their frequencies of occurrence, i.e., quack grass less than 10 percent, smooth brome less than 10 percent, Kentucky bluegrass less than 10 percent, leafy spurge less than 0.01 percent, caragana 0 percent, Russian olive 0 percent, and less than 0.1 percent by other exotic plants (i.e., sweet clover), with the combined total of exotics less than 20 percent on native prairie and reseeded natives.

Strategies:

■ Prescribe burn to reduce undesirable exotics by drying out the soils, eliminating deep (greater than ½ inch) humus layers, and exposing plant growing points to the sun.

■ Reseed greater than or equal to 4,000 acres of croplands (of which about 2,000 acres are in the Lostwood Wilderness Area) to native grasses and forbs.

■ Use grazing and mowing to reduce undesirable exotics where applicable.

■ Use herbicides where needed but keep to a minimum.

■ Use biological controls (i.e., leafy spurge beetles) wherever possible to obtain acceptable control of exotics.

■ Use fire, herbicides, and mechanical methods (i.e., mowing) to eradicate caragana and Russian olive.

Objective D. Manage the biotic integrity of the many indigenous wetland communities.

Strategies:

■ Inventory invertebrate populations for baseline information, and develop a monitoring program to periodically evaluate invertebrate populations that may indicate wetland degradation from pollution (i.e., acid deposition).

■ Monitor wetland flora communities for baseline information.

■ Evaluate effects of defoliation and prolonged rest on wetlands.

Objective E. Manage the Lostwood Wilderness Area's landscape to maintain wilderness values that incorporate indigenous flora and fauna communities.

Strategies:

■ Determine if permission can be gained to reseed about 2,000 acres of croplands to native grasses and forbs using mechanical and chemical tools.

■ Determine how grazing can be used without the use of vehicles.

■ Maintain the use of prescribed burning.

4) Environmental Quality Goal: *Preserve and enhance the pristine quality, wild character, and beauty of a representative sample of the northern Missouri Coteau for the benefit of present and future generations of Americans.*

Objective A. Protect and enhance air, water, and soil resources.

Strategies:

■ Monitor air, water, and soil resources based on current air and water acts to ensure air and water quality is achieved and maintained to assure biological integrity and environmental health.

■ Develop partnerships with appropriate parties (may include petroleum and coal industries) that will ensure the desired quality is maintained.

Objective B. Maintain the integrity of the Lostwood Wilderness Area's integral vista and Class I air quality as required in the Clean Air Act, and native, grassland landscape.

Strategies:

■ Monitor the integral vista and air quality to determine if changes occur and if standards (identified in the Clean Air Act) are being met.

■ Monitor management to evaluate effects on flora and fauna.

■ Restore native grasses and forbs on lands farmed prior and during FWS ownership by reseeding natives, prescribed burning, mowing (if applicable), grazing, and leaving areas rest for up to six years.

■ Renovate and maintain native grasslands using prescribed burning, grazing, and rest.

■ Restore drained wetlands.

■ Eradicate caragana and Russian olive, increasing exotic shrubs, through the use of fire, mechanics, and herbicides.

5) Cultural Resource Goal: *Preserve and interpret the cultural resources of the Lostwood Refuge and surrounding areas for the benefit of present and future generations of Americans.*

Objective A: Maintain archaeological resources and develop interpretation of the native American habitation of the Refuge.

Strategies:

■ After each prescribed burn, search the area for "tipi rings," other native American habitation evidence, and bison "rub rocks."

■ From the prescribed burned searches, have an archaeologist evaluate and record each site, covering about 1/3 of the Refuge every 5 years.

■ Develop an interpretative program that explains the use of the area by native Americans, through such means as the kiosk, brochures, self-guided auto tour, and guided tours.

Objective B: Maintain the archaeological resources and develop interpretation of the early European settler habitation of the Refuge.

Strategies:

■ After each prescribed burn, search the area for sod house foundations.

■ From the prescribed burned searches, have an archaeologist evaluate and record each site, covering about 1/3 of the Refuge every 5 years.

■ Develop an interpretative program that explains the use of the area by early European settlers, through such means as the kiosk, brochures, self-guided auto tour, and guided tours.

6) Public Use Goal: *Nurture an awareness and appreciation of the northern mixed-grass prairie Coteau's wildlife, its ecosystem dynamics, and Refuge management through public involvement, and permitted and compatible public use activities. Through an awareness of Lostwood Refuge, the public will gain an appreciation for the entire Refuge System as the largest system of lands in the world dedicated to wildlife conservation.*

Objective A. Continue and expand where appropriate public hunting of sharp-tailed grouse, gray partridge, and white-tailed deer in conjunction with State laws. (Lostwood Refuge is open to big game and upland game hunting in accordance with State seasons and regulations.)

Strategies:

■ Monitor current and potential recreational users to document desired experiences or changes for each type of hunting season.

■ Maintain existing hunting seasons.

■ Maintain a quality hunt, i.e., a hunting season that permits hunters to hunt designated species but lacks constant disturbance to that species, a disturbance that prevents this species from resuming normal, daily activities.

■ Maintain hunting ethics, taught in most hunter education courses (i.e., respect quarry and its habitat, courteous towards other hunters, safety aspects), through outreach, number of hunters, and enforcement contact and presence.

■ Keep hunting activities compatible with the Refuge System goals and objectives.

■ Determine if other portions of the Refuge can be opened to the hunting of upland game.

Objective B. Develop environmental education and interpretation programs for local school's teachers and students, organized groups (i.e., 4-H, scouts), families, and students of teaching majors (i.e., Minot State University) using any area of Lostwood Refuge that meets lesson plans and management needs.

Strategies:

- Monitor users to document desired experiences or changes for each type of activity.

- Keep the environmental education and interpretation programs dynamic, like the ecosystem the Refuge is within, by using different sites throughout the year, and not using the same sites year after year.

- Construct a learning facility that will provide needed indoor space for education and interpretative programs.

- Develop a variety of Refuge-specific environmental education curriculums, allowing teachers and instructors to conduct self-guided education programs, (i.e., birding, plant, wetland, invertebrate, archaeological, ecological, vertebrate, land management, bio-monitoring, etc.).

- Incorporate within the monthly newspaper articles current Refuge environmental education activities.

- Develop environmental education partnerships with local schools, universities (i.e., Minot State University's teaching curriculum), and organizations.

- Explore ways to make these opportunities available to visitors with disabilities.

Objective C. Develop environmental education and interpretation for Refuge visitors, including birders, hunters, photographers, plant and invertebrate enthusiast, using any area of the Refuge that meets the lesson plans and management needs.

Strategies:

- Monitor users to document desired experiences or changes for each type of activity.

- Keep the environmental education and interpretation programs dynamic, like the ecosystem the Refuge is within, by using different sites throughout the year, and not using the same sites year after year.

- Develop environmental education and interpretative materials for the general public.

- Develop a variety of tours for the general public (i.e., birding, plant, wetland, invertebrate, archaeological, ecological, vertebrate, land management, bio-monitoring, resident and migratory species fall biology).

- Construct a learning facility for indoor interpretative exhibits to orient visitors and help develop an understanding of the Refuge System and Lostwood Refuge and its ecosystem (i.e., wetland and upland habitats displayed with sounds, management and monitoring strategies, hunting regulations, bird watching guides).

- Develop partnerships with instate and out-of-state schools (i.e., intern programs) and organizations.

- Provide monthly news releases discussing items of interest about the Refuge System and Lostwood Refuge.

- Explore ways to make these opportunities available to visitors with disabilities.

Objective D. Maintain and improve opportunities for wildlife observation and photography on Lostwood Refuge.

Strategies:

- Monitor users to document desired experiences or changes for each type of activity.

- Provide fun, family activities (i.e., bird watching, exploring wetlands, looking for insects, discovering plants, archaeological walks, riding horseback, cross-country skiing, North Dakota State Game and Fish's youth deer hunt) that emphasize values of a healthy ecosystem.

- Provide wildlife observation blinds, (i.e., sharp-tailed grouse dancing grounds, wetlands) that are moveable for the varying conditions from year-to-year.

- Present photography ethics to prevent harassment to wildlife, and hints for capturing the beauty and dynamics of grassland flora and fauna, including biology of particular species of interest at the time.

- Maintain a self-guided auto tour route and hiking trail, and year-around hiking and winter snowshoeing and cross-country skiing on the Refuge.

- Make available a portion of the Refuge during a specified time for horseback riding, and give an annual guided horseback tour (horses are not provided).

- Purchase posts for self-guided tours made of material that does not burn.

- Develop special tours during special times of the year (i.e., birding, flowers, grasses [cool and warm seasons], migration, invertebrates).

- Explore ways to make these opportunities available to visitors with disabilities.

7) Research Goal: *Provide a learning platform that will assist management and science to better understand the northern mixed-grass prairie ecosystem that will contribute to conserving and enhancing the quality and diversity of indigenous wildlife.*

Objective A. Develop a unity between management and learning institutions for the common welfare of science, management, and the northern mixed-grass prairie ecosystem.

Strategies:

- Develop intern programs with interested institutions, incorporating a miniature study and applied management opportunities, for the intern.

- Provide opportunities for students to use Lostwood Refuge in pursuit of their education, provided it contributes to further knowledge of the northern mixed-grass prairie.

- Develop a list of potential financial sources that may help students find financial support for their study.

8) Support System Goal: *Interact with communities and organizations to create mutually beneficial partnerships that will accomplish the Refuge System's and the Lostwood Refuge's mission and goals.*

Objective A. Communicate with and engage communities, neighborhoods, and constituencies in the development and implementation of the Refuge Comprehensive Conservation Plan (CCP).

Strategies:

- Develop a list of interested participants.

- Write news releases to local communities within a 100-mile radius of Lostwood Refuge about the CCP.

- Provide an open forum for public comment, both verbal and in writing.

- Develop a Friends Group for Lostwood Refuge.

Objective B. Maintain cooperative agreements with appropriate rural fire departments and State fire Marshall.

Strategies:

- Develop criteria for understanding each party's jurisdiction and restrictions.

- Share in educational/training opportunities.

- Communicate with each rural fire department each year to discuss problems, equipment, burn plans, etc.

Objective C. Develop outreach and partnership programs that are educational and informative of the Refuge System and Lostwood Refuge.

Strategies:

- Identify local civic groups, decisions makers, and organizations interested in a direct line of communication (i.e., news letters to each organization) with the Refuge.

- Provide a special program during the National Wildlife Refuge week to reach as many people and organizations as possible about Refuges being special places.

- Provide monthly news releases discussing items of interest about wildlife, the Refuge System, and Lostwood Refuge.

- Encourage conservation partnerships (i.e., sharing expertise in resource management, providing facilities and assistance in environmental education, attaining air and water quality standards) with Federal and State agencies, organizations, industry, education systems, and the general public to expand compatible benefits for both partners.

- Identify additional methods for outreach and partnerships to increase public knowledge and awareness of wildlife needs, the Refuge System, and Lostwood Refuge.

Habitat Protection Strategy

Several of the Guiding Principles in the 1996 Executive Order express the importance of wildlife diversity in high-quality habitat in several different ways.

- "Fish and wildlife will not prosper without high-quality habitat, and without fish and wildlife, traditional uses of refuges cannot be sustained. The Refuge System will continue to conserve and enhance the quality and diversity of fish and wildlife habitat within refuges . . . to ensure that the biological integrity and environmental health of the Refuge System is maintained for the benefit of present and future generations of Americans . . . ."

Discussions about managing lands for wildlife often emphasizes biospecies diversity. Unfortunately, the approach often taken emphasizes "edge" species, species common across United States, not species requiring large, contiguous habitat units (Samson and Knopf 1982). Samson and Knopf (1982) express:

- "If the ultimate goal of wildlife management is for the optimal maintenance of the total resource, including consumptive, non-consumptive, and esthetic values, the conduct of management should emphasize the type of ecological community mix that will provide assurance of the system maintenance."

Lostwood Refuge is in the northern Great Plains, a subregion comprising all or most of the breeding distribution for several species. The majority of these species receive no emphasis or protection through the Endangered Species Act, even though some have a more restricted range than avian species included in the Endangered Species Act, (i.e., piping plover). Madden (1996) emphasizes the importance of managing this area for species that require large, contiguous habitat.

- "Because the northern Great Plains support several endemic passerines that exist nowhere else (i.e., Baird's sparrow, Sprague's pipit), conservation of habitats used by these species should be emphasized."

Lostwood Refuge is the largest contiguous block of northern mixed-grass prairie in the Prairie Pothole Region under Federal ownership. In managing Lostwood Refuge, we must be careful not to support ". . . widespread species on the edge of their continental range at the expense of regional endemics" (Knopf 1992), but must maintain the open, mixed-grass community so it can contribute to the whole species richness of the natural world.

Because of Lostwood Refuge's location in the Prairie Pothole Region, it is an integral part of a broad coalition of public and private programs that cooperate on international, national, and regional bases to restore and protect wildlife habitat. The Prairie Pothole Region of the U.S. and Canada is North America's premier waterfowl breeding habitat area and the highest priority

Finding an upland sandpiper on a flowering xeric knoll, with Baird's sparrows and Sprague's pipits singing and skylarking around you, butterflies flittering about, and waterfowl slapping the water with their bills as they feed in a nearby wetland, conveys a species richness of not only plants, vertebrates and invertebrates, but also a place of unique beauty, a place that contributes to the richness of the natural world.

of the North American Waterfowl Management Plan (Waterfowl Plan). This Plan was enacted in 1986 among Canada, the U.S., and Mexico to restore waterfowl populations through protection, restoration, and enhancement of wetland and upland habitats. To carry out on-the-ground activities and translate concepts of the Waterfowl Plan, 12 Joint Ventures, including the Prairie Pothole Joint Ventures were established in critical habitat areas of the U.S. and Canada. Joint Ventures are partnerships among Federal, State, and local governments, private landowners, conservation organizations, and the business community to achieve the Waterfowl Plan's waterfowl goals. Because of the associated habitat work, Joint Ventures benefit a broad range of wildlife, including over 300 species of migratory birds.

The Prairie Pothole Joint Venture focuses on two objectives: conserving habitat capable of supporting 6.8 million breeding ducks and an average fall flight of 9.5 million ducks; and stabilizing or increasing populations of declining wildlife species that depend on wetland/grassland complexes, with special emphasis on nongame migratory birds. The Prairie Pothole Joint Venture involves both private and public lands. National Wildlife Refuges, such as Lostwood Refuge, are cornerstones for the Prairie Pothole Joint Venture activities that include wetland and grassland restorations, grassland management, and land acquisition and easements.

In addition to being North American Waterfowl Management Plan's region of highest priority, the Western Hemisphere Shorebird Network recognizes the Prairie Pothole Region as critical breeding and staging habitats for shorebirds. In January 1997, the U.S. portion of the Prairie Pothole Region was again acknowledged for its remarkable wildlife benefits and became the fourth National Conservation Priority Area for the U.S. Department of Agriculture's Conservation Reserve Program.

PLAN IMPLEMENTATION

Strategy for Project Funding and Personnel Requirements

Staffing is needed to conserve and enhance the quality and diversity of indigenous wildlife habitats on Lostwood Refuge. Without proper staffing to implement the habitat management approaches, habitat conditions deteriorate in less than 10 years, changing into a vegetative community that no longer attracts healthy populations of indigenous grassland wildlife.

Appropriate staffing is needed to monitor flora and fauna responses to various management approaches to apply Adaptive Resource Management strategies that are so crucial for long-term success in reaching Lostwood Refuge mission, goals, and objectives. Along with monitoring, research is essential to carefully evaluate management approaches in striving to accomplish Refuge objectives. Refuge staffing is needed to coordinate with research to ensure a final, quality product is obtained. Training and staff is needed for conducting Geographic Information System (GIS) and Global Positioning System (GPS) to take full advantage of modern techniques that will help us frequently evaluate vegetation management through remote sensing and satellite imagery.

Refuge staffing used to conserve and enhance the habitat and monitor responses, have little time and are not properly trained to implement and conduct the wilderness program and the important public relation programs, including environmental education and interpretation, wildlife observation and photography, and other wildlife-dependent recreational activities. If the Service is to be successful in its mission and goals, specially trained staff, with a combination training of public use programs and grassland ecology, is essential. Part of the Refuge staffing that assist both those that conserve and enhance habitat and the public relation programs, are the Refuge maintenance staff, essential staffing if facilities and equipment are to be maintained in a timely manner and meet safety standards. Without all of the permanent staff, as shown in the following section, many of the goals and objectives cannot be attained.

It is extremely important for the refuge manager to keep an open line of communication with staff members, having frequent discussions with all staff to ensure all are working as a team, towards the Lostwood Refuge's goals and objectives. The resource manager must communicate with the public use specialist if the public use staff is going to be able to educate and inform the public about the Refuge management and biological monitoring results. The public use staff must communicate with the resource managers so managers are able to adapt certain management that will help the public use staff to meet their needs. Maintenance staff must understand all staff needs and programs so they can help resolve facility and equipment problems and help wherever they can. Monitoring staff must understand all programs because they must share their information with all staff, and beyond their routine monitoring efforts, they can help in the other programs where needed.

Appropriate funding to pay salaries is essential, as obvious. Equally important are funds to complete routine maintenance and upkeep of facilities and equipment. But, along with this, funding to upgrade and improve facilities and equipment is needed. If we are to expand our knowledge in managing this natural resource, funds must be available to monitor, complete research, apply specific management needs, etc. Without the financial support of the U.S. Government, Lostwood Refuge cannot provide the habitat needed to manage a northern mixed-grass prairie resource for unique, indigenous wildlife. It cannot provide the environmental education and interpretation, and wildlife-dependent recreational activities. Also, it cannot maintain a unique resource for the benefit of present and future generations.

Staffing Plan/Chart

CURRENT, PERMANENT POSITIONS AT THE DES LACS COMPLEX

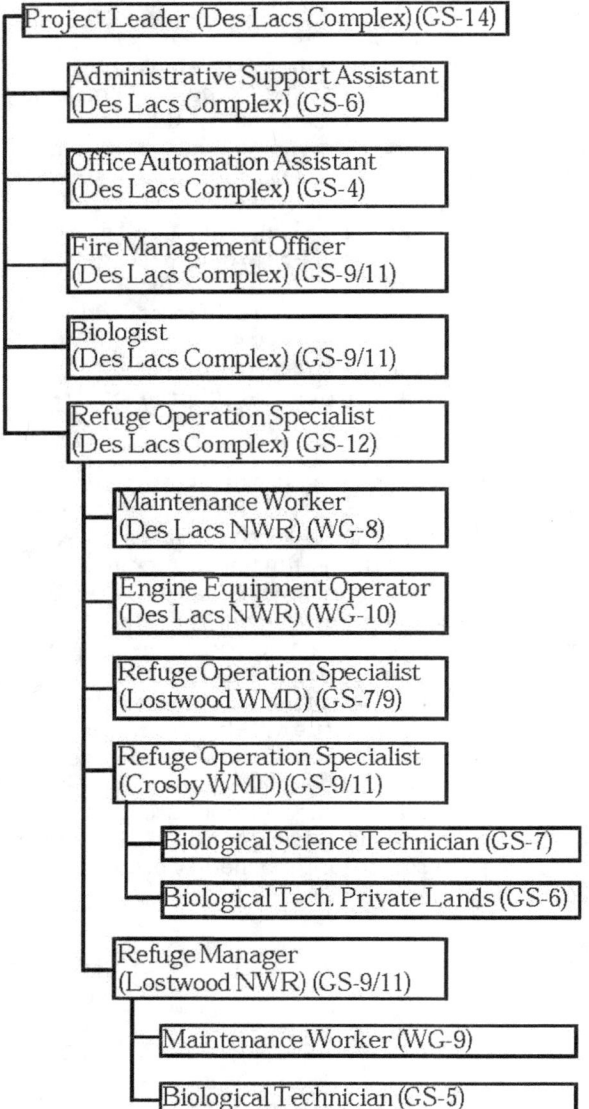

Project Leader (Des Lacs Complex) (GS-14)

Administrative Support Assistant (Des Lacs Complex) (GS-6)

Office Automation Assistant (Des Lacs Complex) (GS-4)

Fire Management Officer (Des Lacs Complex) (GS-9/11)

Biologist (Des Lacs Complex) (GS-9/11)

Refuge Operation Specialist (Des Lacs Complex) (GS-12)

Maintenance Worker (Des Lacs NWR) (WG-8)

Engine Equipment Operator (Des Lacs NWR) (WG-10)

Refuge Operation Specialist (Lostwood WMD) (GS-7/9)

Refuge Operation Specialist (Crosby WMD) (GS-9/11)

Biological Science Technician (GS-7)

Biological Tech. Private Lands (GS-6)

Refuge Manager (Lostwood NWR) (GS-9/11)

Maintenance Worker (WG-9)

Biological Technician (GS-5)

NEEDED STAFFING AT LOSTWOOD REFUGE TO MEET GOALS AND OBJECTIVES

Permanent Employees:

Refuge Manager (GS-11/12)

Assistant Refuge Manager/GIS (GS-9/11)

Biological Technician (GS-5/7)

Maintenance Worker (WG-9)

Maintenance Assistant (WG-6)

Outdoor Recreational Planner (GS-7/9)

Public Use Assistant (Permanent Part Time [PPT]) (GS-4/5/6)

Clerk (PPT) (GS-2/3/4)

Seasonal Employees: ≤ 6 months

2 Biological Technicians GS-2/3/4/5

1 Public Use GS-2/3/4/5

POSITIONS CURRENTLY IDENTIFIED IN RONS

Complex Employees: (divide their time throughout the Complex stations)

Biological Technician (works with piping plover, a threatened species)

Biological Technician (works with the Integrated Pest Management program)

GIS Specialist (works with satellite remote sensing and GIS software and GPS)

Lostwood Refuge Employees: (majority of time spent on Lostwood Refuge)

Clerk, PPT

Outdoor Recreational Planner

Biological Technician (this item, on the Unfunded Operating Needs list, has been accomplished)

Management Plans

More recent plans, guidelines and National Environmental Policy Act (NEPA) requirements that have guided management of Lostwood Refuge are a 1971 "Master Plan," a 1991 "Operating Statement," and a 1994 Environmental Assessment on "Management of Upland Habitats on Lostwood National Wildlife Refuge." The Environmental Assessment for managing upland habitats presented three alternatives: (1) no management, (2) no action, and (3) enhanced management (the preferred alternative), and concluded that no significant impact would exist on the human environment so no Environmental Impact Statement was necessary. Other NEPA requirements met include a 1972 Lostwood Wilderness Area Environmental Impact Statement and a 1984 prescribed burning Environmental Assessment.

Listed below are Management Plans completed (parenthesis indicates years completed) and those needing completion shown in italic.

1. Occupational Safety and Health
* Guidance for Spill Prevention Control and Counter measures (April 1996)
* Safety Plan (September 1991)

2. Wilderness Area Management
* Lostwood Wilderness Management Plan (April 1986)

3. Mineral Management
* Compatibility Plan for Petroleum Exploration and Development (May 1985)

4. Habitat Management Practices
* Wetland Management Plan
 West Rock Slough - Partnership project with Ducks Unlimited
* Grassland and Range Management
Land Use Plan (December 1957)
Grassland Management
* *Integrated Pest Management*
Five-year Pesticide Plan (March 1995)

5. Fire Management
Fire Management Plan (April 1984, March 1995)
Wildfire Management (1984)
National Preparedness Plan (1995)
Annual Prescribed Burning Plans (completed annually)

6. Public Use Management
Hunting (March 1985)
Sign Plan (1987)
Visitor Services and Outreach
Interpretation
Environmental Education

7. Population Management
Wildlife Inventories (1984)
Reintroduction of Selected Species

Partnership Opportunities

Many people --scientist, birders, ranchers, outdoor enthusiasts, horseback riders-- have a great deal of interest in Lostwood Refuge's management and indigenous species. The American Birding Association (ABA) has twice held a major conference in this area for observing unique bird species and learning about grassland management. Numerous Canadian, Federal, and State governments and other organizations have requested tours and to share management ideas about this resource.

Lostwood Refuge has had several partnerships in recent years: the ABA, the National Fish and Wildlife Foundation (NFWF), and currently the Refuge has a funding partnership with The Nature Conservancy for monitoring piping plovers. ABA has expressed interest in funding future grassland passerine studies in the future. The Nature Conservancy has provided financial support for piping plover studies and management. Ducks Unlimited designed and funded a dam on a Refuge natural drainage that created needed waterfowl brood habitat.

Other potential funding partnerships for natural resources and environmental education that need exploring are: World Wildlife Funds, Rocky Mountain Elk Foundation, North Dakota Wetlands Trust, Boise Interagency Fire Center, Wildlife Forever, Mutual of Omaha's Wildlife Heritage Center, The Conservation Fund, Coors Brewing Company, Ducks Unlimited, Mutual of Omaha, Intermodal Surface Transportation Act (develop a Refuge public use road), National Environmental Education and Training Foundation, Toshiba America Foundation, U.S. Environmental Protection Agency's Environmental Education Grants, Fish and Wildlife Service Challenge Cost Share Program, and Biological Resources Division of USGS.

A program called Partners in Flight, launched by the NFWF, strives to "... improve our understanding of Neotropical migrants, identify species most at risk, and develop and carry out cooperative plans to protect their habitat." The Refuge staff can develop partnerships with Partners in Flight for assistance in accomplishing specific monitoring objectives. Potential partnerships, identified in a Partners in Flight publication, are: Colorado Bird Observatory, Cornell Laboratory of Ornithology, Defenders of Wildlife, Long Point Bird Observatory, Manomet Observatory for Conservation Sciences, National Audubon Society, National Wildlife Federation, and Point Reyes Bird Observatory (Citizen's Guide to Migratory Bird Conservation, 1995).

Partnerships require extensive Refuge time to coordinate and develop. Without appropriate staffing, time spent in finding and developing partnerships is time lost to improve and maintain habitat. The end result is the habitat on the land degrades. More staffing is needed if we are to get out of this "rut" so we can expand our partnerships and accomplish more with the time and funds available.

More people need to be exposed to the Refuge System through Outreach. The Refuge has and will continue to complete partnerships with: livestock operators; rural fire departments (Powers Lake, Bowbells, and Stanley); Interagency Fire Teams; Universities and Colleges (University of Stevens Point, University of Missouri, North Dakota State University, University of North Dakota, Montana State University, University of Montana, Minot State University, and South Dakota State University); National Biological Service; ABA; The Nature Conservancy; NFWF; and other refuges (i.e., such projects as the recovery of the piping plover). New partnerships can be formed with other resource interested organizations, local civic groups for environmental education and interpretation (i.e., 4-H, scouts), community schools (four local), Federal and State governments, and other civic organizations and events (i.e., Goose Fest).

Monitoring and Evaluation

Throughout this Plan, the importance of monitoring and evaluating effects of management on flora and fauna are critical in measuring progress towards attaining goals and objectives. This requires permanent and seasonal staffing, and help from volunteers if we are to correctly apply ARM procedures. Also, it requires personnel to become knowledgeable and use the new, broadening fields of GIS and GPS. These new tools will help make flora assessments much broader and complete for long-term vegetation monitoring with fewer observation errors.

To determine if we are achieving our objectives, monitoring of species groups for each type of defoliation event (i.e., grazing, prescribed burning, mowing) and rest (no defoliation) in specific habitat types (native grasslands, reseeded natives, old cropland, and wetlands) is needed. Species groups include passerines, waterfowl, raptors, microtines, canids, and key species of invertebrates. Monitoring techniques have been developed for many of the species groups, although improvement is needed; however, not all species groups in all defoliation events have been monitored. Limited staffing and volunteers have slowed development and implementation of monitoring and evaluation programs.

Vegetation changes slowly over several years. To achieve the flora objectives, monitoring each type of defoliation event (i.e., grazing, prescribed burning, mowing) and rest (no defoliation) in native grasslands, reseeded natives, old cropland, and wetlands about every 3-5 years is needed. The desire is to use satellite imagery and ground-truthing through GIS programs and GPS; however, if this is not available, a laborious, time-consuming task of plant transects must be undertaken by a botanist. Plant community types need to be identified for similar soil types and topography.

Piping plover, the only U.S. Threatened or Endangered species that reproduces on the Refuge, needs improved shoreline habitat, protection from predators, and individual birds should be monitored until they depart. Other species in the Endangered Species program, bald eagles, peregrine falcon, and whooping cranes, are present only during migration, but individuals need to be periodically monitored when present.

APPENDIX A

References and Bibliography

Anderson, H.G., and A.W. Bailey. 1980. Effects of annual burning on grassland in the Aspen Parkland of east-central Alberta. Can. J. Bot. 58(8):985-996.

Anderson, M. L., and A. W. Bailey. 1979. Effect of fire on a Symphoricarpos occidentalis shrub community in central Alberta. Can. J. Bot. 57:2819-2823.

Bailey, A.W. 1988. Understanding fire ecology for range management. *In* Vegetation science applications for rangeland analysis and management, P.T. Tueller, editor. Kluwer Academic Publishers, Dordrecht, Boston, London.

Barbour, M. G., J. H. Burk, and W. D. Pitts. 1980. Terrestrial plant ecology. Benjamin/Cummings Publ. Co., Inc., Menlo Park, Calif. 604pp.

Beintema, A. J., H. R. J. Beintema, and G. J. D. M. Muskens. 1985. A shift in the timing of breeding in meadow birds. Ardea 73:83-89.

Bentivenga, S. P., and B. A. D. Hetrick. 1992. The effect of prairie management practices on mycorrhizal symbiosis. Mycologia 84:522-527.

Bird, R. D. 1971. Ecology of the aspen parkland of western Canada in relation to land use. Can. Dep. Agric. Contrib. No. 27. 155pp.

Biondini, M. E., A. A. Steuter, C. E. Grygiel. 1989. Seasonal fire effects on the diversity patterns, spatial distribution and community structure of forbs in the northern mixed grass prairie, USA. Vegetation 85, 21-31.

Bluemle, J. P. 1977. The face of North Dakota: the geologic story. North Dakota Geol. Surv. Educ. Ser. 11. 73pp.

Bollinger, E. K., P. B. Bollinger, and T. A. Gavin. 1990. Effects of hay-cropping on eastern populations of the bobolink. Wildl. Soc. Bull. 18:142-150.

Bowen, B. S., and A. D. Kruse. 1993. Effects of grazing on nesting by upland sandpipers in southcentral North Dakota. J. Wildl. Manage. 57:291-301.

Bragg, T.B. 1995. Climate, soils and fire: The physical environment of North American grasslands. *In* The Changing Prairie, K. Keeler and A. Joern, editors. Oxford University Press, NY.

_____ and A.A. Steuter. 1996. Prairie ecology--The mixed prairie. *In* Prairie Conservation, F.B. Samson, and F.L. Knopf, editors. Island Press, CA.

Burgess, H. H., H. H. Prince, and D. L. Trauger. 1965. Blue-winged teal nesting success as related to land use. J. wildl. Manage. 29:89-95.

Clayton, L. 1967. Stagnant-glacier features of the Missouri Coteau in North Dakota. North Dakota Geol. Surv. Misc. Ser. 30:24-46.

Coleman, D. C., C. P. P. Reid, and C. V. Cole. 1983. Biological strategies of nutrient cycling in soil systems. Pages 1-55 *in* A. MacFadyen and E. D. Foral, eds. Advances in ecological research, vol. 13. Academic Press.

Coupland, R. T. 1950. Ecology of mixed prairie in Canada. Ecol. Monogr. 20:271-315.

_____ 1961. A reconsideration of grassland classification in the northern Great Plains of North America. J. Ecol. 49:135-167.

Coyne, P.L., M.J. Trlica, and C.E. Owensby. 1995. Carbon and nitrogen dynamics in range plants. Pages 59-167. *in* D.J. Bedunah and R.E. Sosebee (eds). Wildland plants: physiological ecology and developmental morphology. Soc. for Range Manage. Denver.

Denig, E. T. 1961. Five Indian tribes of the upper Missouri. Univ. Oklahoma Press, Norman, OK.

Duebbert, H. F. 1969. High nest density and hatching success of ducks on South Dakota CAP land. Trans. North Am. Wildl. Nat. Resour. Conf. 34:218-228.

_____ and H. A. Kantrud. 1974. Upland duck nesting related to land use and predator reduction. J. Wildl. Manage. 38:257-265.

Eadie, W. R. 1953. Response of Microtus to vegetative cover. J. Mammal. 34:263-264.

Edwards, T. 1978. Buffalo and prairie ecology. Proc. Midwest Prairie Conf. 5:110-112.

Ellison, L. 1960. The influence of grazing on plant succession of rangelands. Bot. Rev. 26:1-78.

Freers, T. F. 1973. Geology of Burke County, North Dakota. North Dakota Geol. Surv. Bull. 55. 32pp.

Federal Geographic Data Committee, Vegetation Subcommittee. 1996. FGDC Vegetation Classification and Information Standards. USGS MS 590 National Center, 12201 Sunrise Valley Drive, Reston, VA 22092. 27pp.

Freers, T. F. 1973. Geology of Burke County, North Dakota. North Dakota Geol. Surv. Bull. 55 32 pp.

Gates, J. M. 1965. Duck nesting and production on Wisconsin farmlands. J. Wildl. Manage. 29:515-523.

Gjersing, F. M. 1975. Waterfowl production in relation to rest-rotation grazing. J. Range Manage. 28:37-42.

Grinell, G. B. 1970. Last of the buffalo. Arno Press, New York.

Haug, E. A., and L. W. Oliphant. 1990. Movements, activity patterns, and habitat use of burrowing owls in Saskatchewan. J. Wildl. Manage. 54:27-35.

Higgins, K. F. 1986. Interpretation and compendium of historical fire accounts in the northern Great Plains. U.S. Fish Wildl. Serv. Resour. Publ. 161. 39pp.

_____ and W. T. Barker. 1982. Changes in vegetation structure in seeded nesting cover in the prairie pothole region. U.S. Fish Wildl. Serv. Spec. Sci. Rep. Wildl. 242. 26pp.

_____, H. F. Duebbert, and R. B. Oetting. 1969. Nesting of the upland plover on the Missouri Coteau. Prairie Nat. 1:45-48.

_____, A. D. Kruse, and J. L. Piehl. 1989. Prescribed burning guidelines in the northern Great Plains. South Dakota State Univ. Ext. Circ. No. 760. 36pp.

Hornaday, W. T. 1889. The extermination of the American bison, Vol. 2. Annu. Rep. Smithsonian Inst. (1887), Washington, D.C.

Houston, C. S., and M. J. Bechard. 1983. Trees and the red-tailed hawk in southern Saskatchewan. Blue Jay 41:99-109.

_____, and M. J. Bechard. 1984. Decline of the ferruginous hawk in Saskatchewan. Am. Birds 38:166-170.

Huber, G. E., and A. A. Steuter. 1984. Vegetation profile and grassland bird response to spring burning. Prairie Nat. 16:55-61.

Hulbert, L. C. 1969. Fire and litter effects in undisturbed bluestem prairie in Kansas. Ecology 50:874-877.

Jasikoff, T. M. 1982. Habitat suitability index models: ferruginous hawk. U.S. Fish Wildl. Serv. Biol. Rep. FWS/OBS-82/10.10. 18pp.

Joyce, L. A., and M. D. Skold. 1988. Implications of changes in the regional ecology of the Great Plains. U.S. For. Serv. Gen. Tech. Rep. RM-158:115-127.

Johnson, D.H., A.B Sargeant, R.J. Greenwood. 1989. Importance of individual species of predators on nesting success of ducks in the Canadian Prairie Pothole Region. Can. J. Zool. 67, 291-297.

Kaiser, P. H., S. S. Berlinger, and L. H. Fredrickson. 1979. Response of blue-winged teal to range management on waterfowl production areas in southeastern South Dakota. J. Range Manage. 32:295-298.

Kantrud, H. A. 1981. Grazing intensity effects on the breeding avifauna of North Dakota native grass lands. Can. Field-Nat. 95:404-417.

_____, and K. F. Higgins. 1992. Nest and nest site characteristics of some ground-nesting, non-passerine birds of northern grasslands. Prairie Nat. 24:67-84.

_____, and R. L. Kologiski. 1983. Avian associations of the northern Great Plains grassland. J. Biogeogr. 10:331-350.

_____, G. L. Krapu, and G. A. Swanson. 1989. Prairie basin wetlands of the Dakotas: a community profile. U.S. Fish Wildl. Serv. Biol. Rep. 85. 111pp.

Keith, L.B. 1961. A study of waterfowl ecology on small impoundments in southeastern Albert. Wildl. Monogr. 6, 1-88.

Kellogg, R. 1915. North Dakota: Lostwood, Mountrail County. Unpubl. U.S. Biol. Surv. Notes, Smithsonian Inst. Archives, Record Unit 7176, Washington, D.C.

Kemner, D. P. 1989. Response by upland nesting birds to three rejuvenation treatments applied to two types of seeded nesting cover in eastern South Dakota. M.S. Thesis. S. Dakota State Univ., Brookings.

Kirby, R. E., J.K. Ringleman, D.R. Anderson, R.S. Sojda. 1992. Grazing on National Wildlife Refuges: do the needs outweigh the problems? Trans. North Am. Wildl. Nat. Resourc. Conf. 57, 611-626.

Kirsch, L. M. 1969. Waterfowl production in relation to grazing. J. Wildl. Manage. 33:821-828.

_____, and A. D. Kruse. 1973. Prairie fires and wildlife. Proc. Tall Timbers Fire Ecol. Conf. 12:289-303.

_____, H. F. Duebbert, and A. D. Kruse. 1978. Grazing and haying effects on habitats of upland nesting birds. Trans. N. Am. Wildl. Nat. Resour. Conf. 43:486-497.

Knopf, F. L. 1992. Faunal mixing, faunal integrity, and the biopolitical template for diversity conservation. Transactions of the North American Wildlife and Natural Resources Conference 57:330-342.

Konrad, P. M., and D. S. Gilmer. 1984. Observations on the nesting ecology of burrowing owls in central North Dakota. Prairie Nat. 16:129-130.

Kotler, B. P., M. S. Gaines, and B. J. Danielson. 1988. The effects of vegetative cover on the community structure of prairie rodents. Acta Theriol. 33:379-392.

Kruse, A. D., and B. Bowen. 1996. Effects of grazing and burning on densities and habitats of nesting ducks in North Dakota. J. Wildl. Manage. 60:233-246.

_____, and J.L. Piehl. 1986. The impact of prescribed burning on ground nesting birds. Proc. North Am. Prairie Conf. 9, 153-156.

LaBaugh, J. W. 1986. Wetland ecosystem studies from a hydrologic perspective. Am. Water Resour. Asso. Bull. 22. 10pp.

Labisky, R. F. 1957. Relation of hay harvesting system to duck nesting under a refuge-permittee system. J. Wildl. Manage. 21:194-200.

Larson, F. 1940. The role of bison in maintaining the short grass plains. Ecology 21:113-121.

Lemen, C. A., and M. K. Clausen. 1984. The effects of mowing on the rodent community of a native tallgrass prairie in eastern Nebraska. Prairie Nat. 16:5-10.

LoBue, J., and R. M. Darnell. 1959. Effect of habitat disturbance on a small mammal population. J. Mammal. 40:425-437.

Luttschwager, K. A., and K. F. Higgins. 1991. Some sociological and ecological effects of the Conservation Reserve Program in the Northern Great Plains. U.S. For. Serv. Gen. Tech. Rep. RM-203:58-62.

Madden, E. M. 1996. Passerine communities and bird-habitat relationships on prescribe-burned, mixed-grass prairie in North Dakota. Master Dissertation. Montana State University, Bozeman.

Maher, W.J. 1973. Birds. I. Population dynamics. Tech. Rep. 34, Can. Comm. Internat. Biol. Program, Univ. Saskatchewan, Saskatoon. 56 pp.

Maini, J.S. 1960. Invasion of grassland by Populus tremuloides in the Northern Great Plains. Ph.D. Thesis, Univ. Saskatchewan, Saskatoon. 231pp.

Manske, L. L. 1994. Ecological management of grass-lands defoliation. Pages 130-136. in Taha, R.K., Z. Abouguendia, and P.R. Horton eds. Managing Canadian rangelands for sustainability and profit ability. Grazing and Pasture Tech. Program, Regina, Saskatchewan.

_____. 1996. Adaptive tolerance mechanisms in grass plants. Pages 97-99. in Z. Abouguendia, ed. Total Ranch Management in the Northern Great Plains. Grazing and Pasture Tech. Program, Saskatchewan Agriculture and Food. Regina, Saskatchewan.

Martz, G. F. 1967. Effects of nesting cover removal on breeding puddle ducks. J. Wildl. Manage. 31:236-247.

McGowan, K. J., and T. A. Bookhout. 1986. Small mammal populations on Ohio (USA) strip mined lands reclaimed with herbaceous vegetation under old and new reclamation laws. Ohio J. Sci. 86:29-32.

Messmer, T. A. 1985. Effects of specialized grazing systems on upland nesting birds. M.S. Thesis. North Dakota State Univ., Fargo.

Miller, H. W. 1971. Relationships of duck nesting success to land use in North and South Dakota. Trans. Congr. Int. Union Game Biol. 10:133-140.

Mundinger, J. G. 1976. Waterfowl response to rest-rotation grazing. J. Wildl. Manage. 40:60-68.

Murphy, R. K. 1993. History, nesting biology, and predation ecology of raptors in the Missouri Coteau of northwestern North Dakota. Ph.D. Dissertation. Montana State University, Bozeman.

Newton, I. 1979. Population ecology of raptors. Buteo Books, Vermillion, South Dakota. 399pp.

North Dakota Department of Agriculture. 1993. North Dakota's noxious weed law. North Dakota Dep. Agric. 22pp.

Ode, D.J, et al. 1980. The seasonal contribution of C3 and C4 plant species to primary production in a mixed prairie. Ecology. 61:1304-11.

Oetting, R. B., and J. F. Cassel. 1971. Waterfowl nesting on interstate highway right-of-way in North Dakota. J. Wildl. Manage. 35:774-781.

Owens, R. A., and M. T. Myers. 1973. Effects of agriculture upon populations of native passerine birds of an Alberta fescue grassland. Can. J. Zool. 51:697-713

Page, R. D., and J. F. Cassel. 1971. Waterfowl nesting on a railroad right-of-way in North Dakota. J. Wildl. Manage. 35:544-549.

Pelton, J. 1953. Studies on the life history of Symphoricarpos occidentalis Hook. in Minnesota. Ecol. Monogr. 23:17-39.

Pfeifer, R., and R. Brandl. 1991. The timing of meadow mowing and its influence on birds. Ornithologischer Anzeiger 30:159-171.

Ryan, M. R. 1990. A dynamic approach to the conservation of the prairie ecosystem in the Midwest. Pages 91-106 in J. M. Sweeney, ed. Management of dynamic ecosystems. North Cent. Sect., The Wildl. Soc., West Lafayette, Ind.

_____, and R. B. Renken. 1987. Habitat use by breeding willets in the Northern Great Plains. Wilson Bull. 99:175-189.

_____, R. B. Renken, and J. J. Dinsmore. 1984. Marbled godwit habitat selection in the northern prairie region. J. Wildl. Manage. 48:1206-1218.

_____, B. G. Root, and P. M. Mayer. 1993. Status of piping plovers in the Great Plains of North America: a demographic simulation model. Conserv. Biol. 7:581-585.

Samson, F. B., and F. L. Knopf. 1982. In search of a diversity ethic for wildlife management. Trans. North Am. Wildl. Nat. Resourc. Conf. 47:421-431.

Sauer, C. O. 1950. Grassland climax, fire, and man. J. Range Manage. 3:16-21.

Sawhill, J. C. 1996. Intimate landscapes, transcendent issues. The Nature Conservancy. September/October, p.5.

Schmutz, J. K. 1984. Ferruginous and Swainson's hawk abundance and distribution in relation to land use in southeastern Alberta. J. Wildl. Manage. 48:1180-1187.

_____, S. M. Schmutz, and D. A. Boag. 1980. Coexistence of three species of hawks (Buteo spp.) in the prairie-parkland ecotone. Can. J. Zool. 58:1075-1079.

Sedivec, K. K., T. A. Messmer, W. T. Barker, K. F. Higgins, and D. R. Hertel. 1990. Nesting success of upland nesting waterfowl and sharp-tailed grouse in specialized grazing systems in southcentral North Dakota. U.S. For. Serv. Gen. Rep. RM-194:71-92.

Sharp, B. 1986. Management guidelines for the Swainson's hawk. U.S. Fish Wildl. Serv. Region 1, Portland, Oregon. unpubl. rep.

Singh, J. S., W. K. Lauenroth, R. K. Heitschmidt, and J. L. Dodd. 1983. Structural and functional attributes of the vegetation of northern mixed prairie of North America. Bot. Rev. 49:117-149.

Sousa, P. J., and W. N. McDonal. 1983. Habitat suitability models: Baird's sparrow. U.S. Fish Wildl. Serv. FWS/OBS 82/10.44:12pp.

Sovada, M. A., A. B. Sargeant, and F. W. Grier. 1995. Differential effects of coyotes and red foxes on duck nest success. J. Wildl. Manage. 59:1-9.

Steuter, A. A., C. E. Grygiel, M. E. Biondini. 1990. A synthesis approach to management planning and the conceptual development and implementation. Nat. Areas. J. 10, 61-68.

Strassman, B. I. 1987. Effects of cattle grazing and haying on wildlife conservation at National Wildlife Refuges in the USA. Environ. Manage. 11(1), 35-44.

Stoddart, L. A., A. D. Smith, and T. W. Box. 1975. Range management, 3rd ed. McGraw-Hill, New York.

Stubbendieck, J. 1988. Historical development of native vegetation on the Great Plains. U.S. For. Serv. Gen. Tech. Rep. RM-158:21-28.

Toland, B. R. 1986. Nesting ecology of northern harriers in southwest Missouri. Trans. Mo. Acad. Sci. 20:49-57.

U.S. Fish and Wildlife Service 1994. Management of upland habitat on Lostwood National Wildlife Refuge. Unpublished Environmental Assessment, Denver, CO.

U.S. Soil Conservation Service. 1975. Field technical guide: Coteau vegetation zone. U.S. Dep. Agric., Soil Conserv. Serv., North Dakota. 14pp.

Vogl, R. J. 1967. Controlled burning for wildlife in Wisconsin. Proc. Tall Timbers Fire Ecol. Conf. 6:47-96.

_____ 1974. Effects of fire on grasslands. Pages 139-194 in T. T. Kozlowski and C. E. Ahlgren, eds. Fire and ecosystems. Academic Press, New York.

Voorhees, L. D., and J. F. Cassel. 1980. Highway right-of-way: mowing versus succession as related to duck nesting. J. Wildl. Manage. 44:155-163.

Wakeley, J. S. 1978. Factors affecting the use of hunting sites by ferruginous hawks. Condor 80:316-326.

Wallace, L. L. 1987. Effects of clipping and soil compaction on growth, morphology and mycorrhizal colonization of Schizachyrium scoparium, a C4 bunchgrass. Oecologia 72:423-428.

Walters, C. 1986. Adaptive management of renewable resources. MacMillan Publishing Company, New York. 374 pp.

Wettlaufer, B. N., and W. J. Mayer-Oakes. 1960. The Long Creek site. Sask. Mus. Nat. Hist. Anthropol. Ser. No. 2

Wiens, J. A. 1970. Habitat heterogeneity and the structure of avian communities in grasslands. Bull. Ecol. Soc. Am. Suppl. 51:29. abstract only.

Winter, T. C. 1989. Hydrologic studies of wetlands in the northern prairie. Pages 16-54 in A. G. van der Valk, ed. Northern prairie wetlands. Iowa State Univ. Press, Ames, Iowa.

Wright, H. A., and A. W. Bailey. 1982. Fire ecology. J. Wiley and Sons, New York.

APPENDIX B

Glossary of Terms

Animal Impact. This is the sum total of all the direct physical influences of livestock on grasslands such as trampling, dunging, urinating, salivating, rubbing, digging, etc. Animal impact is controlled through stock density and time.

Animal Unit Month (AUM). An AUM is the amount of forage necessary to maintain one 1,000-pound animal for 1 month.

Cool Season Grasses. These grasses have a C_3 photosynthetic process (Barbour *et al.* 1980). Optimum growth of cool season grasses is approximately 50° to 77° F (Coyne *et al.* 1995). On Lostwood Refuge, their primary growth periods are spring (May-June) and fall (September). Examples of native, cool season grasses are green needlegrass, western wheatgrass, and needle-and-thread.

Cool Season Exotic Grasses. These are cool season grasses that are not native to North America. They also may be referred to as introduced or tame grasses, and examples include smooth brome, quackgrass, intermediate wheatgrass, and tall wheatgrass. Kentucky bluegrass is included in this group, however, it was likely native in North America but probably not in northwestern North Dakota.

Defoliation. Removal of live and residual vegetation by various management methods, i.e., grazing, mowing, burning.

Deteriorated (poor condition). As applied to grasslands in this CCP, refers to a condition of less-than-potential total biotic productivity as a result of environmental conditions not natural to the site. Deteriorated grasslands typically have low species diversity (plant and animal), poor plant vigor, large quantities of matted litter, and significant proportions of undesirable plant species.

Endemic. Native to or restricted to a particular area or region.

Grazing. Feeding on grasses and other herbage by domestic livestock.

Grassland Succession. The process of change and development in the entire grassland community. See also high succession.

Haying. Mechanical harvest of grasses and other herbage for livestock feed.

High Succession (or high successional stage). Relatively complex, stable communities composed of populations of many different species of plants, animals, birds, insects, and microorganisms. Usually highly stable in that populations of member species tend to replace themselves over time and are resilient to perturbations. See also succession, below.

High Grassland Succession. Complex grassland communities composed of populations of a great many different species of plants, animals, birds, insects, and microorganisms. Usually highly stable and not prone to high fluctuations in numbers of individual populations. See also succession.

Indigenous. Occurring or living historically in a geographic area. Synonymous with native species.

Indigenous Migratory Birds. Migratory birds occurring or living historically on Lostwood Refuge. "Synonymous with native, migratory bird species."

Litter. Residual vegetation that has lodged and become matted.

Low Succession. Simple communities composed of populations of only a few species. Usually highly unstable and vulnerable to fluctuations. See also succession.

Low Grassland Succession. Simple grassland communities composed of populations of only a few species. Usually highly unstable and vulnerable to fluctuations. See also succession.

Maintenance. Grassland management phase where the habitat is alternately burned and grazed with 2-5 year rest periods.

Mowing. Mechanical cutting of grasses and herbage without the removal of the cut grasses and herbage.

Outreach. A program developed by the Fish and Wildlife Service to help the public become aware of the Service and perhaps create understanding and support.

Prescribed Burning. Controlled application of fire to wildland fuels in either their natural or modified state, under such conditions, as to allow the fire to be confined to a predetermined area while producing the intensity of heat and rate of spread required to achieve planned management objectives.

Renovation. Grassland management phase involving burning three times over 5-7 years to reduce woody plants, and restore native plants to the grassland.

Renovation-Maintenance. Grassland management phase involving a combination of the following tools; 3 years of grazing, rest for 2-3 years, and spring burn 1-2 times over approximately 7 years depending on conditions.

Residual Vegetation. Upright dead vegetation remaining from previous years of growth. Residual vegetation is different from litter in that it has not lodged.

Stocking Density. The relationship between number of animals and area of land at any instant of time, expressed in this document as animal-units per acre (AU/ac).

Stocking rate. The number of specific kinds and classes of animals grazing a unit of land for a specified time period, expressed in this document as animal unit months per acre (AUM/ac).

Succession. The orderly and predictable process of change and development in a biotic community, involving interactions among abiotic factors, microorganisms, plants, and animals. Procession is from simple communities composed of few species to diverse communities with complex interactions. Stability, the inherent resilience of populations within the community to change, generally increases as succession proceeds forward (Odum 1971) although exceptions do exist (Odum 1969). A tendency towards balanced production:respiration ratios also exists. Succession may potentially reach a "climax" community type for a given geographic area; the climax is composed of populations of species that tend to replace themselves, instead of continuing to change to a community of different composition. The concept of succession in northern Great Plains grasslands under pristine i.e., pre-settlement conditions (i.e., in the 1800's) is less clear than traditional examples such as oak-hickory forest as a climax type of the eastern U.S. In the northern Great Plains, a climax type or "high succession" state is one characterized by repeated, catastrophic disturbances especially fire, bison grazing, and drought. Even though the grassland community historically was frequently altered by such events, it was composed of populations of characteristic plant and animal species that were dynamic in a given place over several years, but apparently were relatively stable over decades or centuries. Thus, in this document, "high succession" conveys close proximity to the pristine condition (even though this is not clearly defined), and thus a high degree of ecological integrity.

Warm Season Grasses. These grasses have a C_4 photosynthetic process (Barbour *et al.* 1980). Optimum growth of warm season grasses is 86° to 105° F (Coyne *et al.* 1995). On Lostwood Refuge, their primary growth period is in summer (late June-August). Examples may include switchgrass, big bluestem, little bluestem, and plains muhly.

APPENDIX C

Compatibility Determination

Compatibility Determinations prepared for the 1994 Environmental Assessment entitled "Management of Upland Habitats on Lostwood National Wildlife Refuge" follow.

All other uses have current compatibility determinations that are filed at Lostwood Refuge and are available for public inspection. All compatibility determinations will be reviewed and updated as appropriate.

STATION NAME: Lostwood National   DATE ESTABLISHED: September 4, 1935
                 Wildlife Refuge

ESTABLISHING AND ACQUISITION AUTHORITIES:

Lostwood National Wildlife Refuge, located in Burke and Mountrail Counties, North Dakota, was established on September 4, 1935 by Executive Order. Additional lands within the refuge boundary were acquired through the Migratory Bird Conservation Act.

PURPOSE(S) FOR WHICH ESTABLISHED:

Lostwood National Wildlife Refuge was established "... as a refuge and breeding ground for migratory birds an other wildlife:..." Executive Order 7171, dated September 4, 1935 and "... for use as an inviolate sanctuary, or for any other management purpose, of migratory birds." 16 U.S.C. 715d (Migratory Bird Conservation Act) and for "... the conservation of the wetlands of the Nation in order to maintain the public benefits they provide and to help fulfill international obligations contained in various migratory bird treaties and conventions ..." 16 U.S.C. 3901(b), 100 Stat. 3583 (Emergency Wetlands Resources Act of 1986)

APPLICABLE LAWS, REGULATIONS AND POLICIES:

National Wildlife Refuge Administration Act of 1966 as amended (16 U.S.C. 668dd-668ee), Refuge Recreation Act of 1962 as amended (16 U.S.C. 460k-460k-4)

DESCRIPTION OF PROPOSED USE:

Manage upland habitats on Lostwood National Wildlife Refuge following the preferred alternative in an Environmental Assessment of Management of Upland Habitats on Lostwood National Wildlife Refuge, North Dakota.

1

ANTICIPATED IMPACTS ON SERVICE LANDS, WATERS OR INTERESTS:

The preferred management alternative described in the attached Environmental Assessment of Management of Upland Habitats on Lostwood National Wildlife Refuge, North Dakota is designed solely to achieve the objectives and purposes for which this refuge was established. Thus, implementation of this alternative will, within available funding levels, result in the most productive habitat possible for migratory birds, endangered species and most other species of wildlife indigenous to Northwestern North Dakota.

Some short term, negative impacts will result from implementation of the preferred alternative:

1. Defoliation techniques will temporarily decrease suitability of nesting habitat for those species dependent on dense nesting cover.

2. Tracts undergoing farming treatments will have an increased probability of soil erosion during the cropping and grass establishment phase.

3. Some waterfowl nests will not be initiated in tracts receiving grazing treatment.

DETERMINATION: (CHECK ONE)

This use is compatible.   X   This use is not compatible. _____

THE FOLLOWING STIPULATIONS ARE REQUIRED TO ENSURE COMPATIBILITY:

1) All management tools used must follow the prescription developed for treatment of each specific tract of land.

2) Cultivation to establish native grass stands will be used as a last resort after less radical measures have failed to meet management objectives.

3) Farming practices will comply with high soil conservation standards.

4) Temporary fencing will be used to the maximum extent possible (other than boundary fences) to control livestock, minimizing entanglement problems with deer.

2

5) Vegetation and nesting phenology will both be used to determine defoliation treatments (i.e. grazing, haying, burning) on specific tracts.

JUSTIFICATION:

Implementation of the preferred alternative described in the Environmental Assessment of Management of Upland Habitats on Lostwood National Wildlife Refuge will not materially interfere with or detract from the purposes for which this refuge was established. This alternative presents the best plan available to meet these purposes.

PROJECT LEADER: MICHAEL D. BLENDEN   July 7, 1994
NAME/SIGNATURE/DATE

REVIEW AND CONCURRENCE: Ronald Shupe, Refuge Supervisor   9/8/94
for NAME/TITLE/SIGNATURE/DATE

Review and Concurrence: Wilbur Ladd, Assistant Regional Director (RW)   9/13/94
NAME/TITLE/SIGNATURE/DATE

Supporting Documents Attached ___Y___

IF ADDITIONAL SPACE IS REQUIRED, ATTACH CONTINUATION SHEETS.

3

UNITED STATES FISH AND WILDLIFE SERVICE

ENVIRONMENTAL ACTION MEMORANDUM

Within the spirit and intent of the Council on Environmental Quality's regulations for implementing the National Environmental Policy Act (NEPA) and other statutes, orders, and policies that protect fish and wildlife resources, I have established the following administrative record and have determined that the action of Upland Management of Lostwood National Wildlife Refuge:

_____ is a categorical exclusion as provided by 516 DM 6 Appendix 1. No further documentation will be made (see instructions on back).

___X___ is found not to have significant environmental effects as determined by the attached Environmental Assessment and Finding of No Significant Impact.

_____ is found to have special environmental conditions as described in the attached Environmental Assessment. The attached Findings of No Significant Impact will not be final nor any actions taken pending 30-day period for public review (40 CFR 1501.4(e)(2)).

_____ is found to have significant effects, and therefore a "Notice of Intent" will be published in the Federal Register to prepare an Environmental Impact Statement before the project is considered further.

_____ is denied because of environmental damage, Service policy, or mandate.

_____ is an emergency situation. Only those actions necessary to control the immediate impacts of the emergency will be taken. Other related actions remain subject to NEPA review.

Other supporting documents:

Management of Upland Habitats on Lostwood National Wildlife Refuge Environmental Assessment and Finding of No Significant Impact.

		NA	
		Director/Regional Director	Date
Michael Blenden 5/6/94		*Maurice Burright 9/8/94*	
Initiator	Date	PM/ARD	Date
NA		*NA*	
**	Date	EC/REC	Date

* - as delegated by 4 AM 4.1 Director Order No. 5
** - for Special Review (see Instructions)

APPENDIX D

Intra-Service Section 7 Evaluation

INTRA-SERVICE SECTION 7 EVALUATION

REGION: 6   Mountain-Prairie

PROGRAM: National Wildlife Refuge Comprehensive Conservation Planning

PROJECT: Lostwood National Wildlife Refuge Comprehensive Conservation Plan

LOCATION: Lostwood National Wildlife Refuge, Burke and Mountrail Counties, North Dakota

LISTED SPECIES THAT COULD BE AFFECTED:

Piping plover (*Charadrius melodus*)
Bald eagle (*Haliaeetus leucocephalus*)
Peregrine falcon (*Falco peregrinus*)
Whooping crane (*Grus americana*)

NAME AND DESCRIPTION OF THE ACTION:

Through implementation of the Comprehensive Conservation Plan, Lostwood National Wildlife Refuge staff will be working to restore and preserve the indigenous biological communities of the mid to late 1800's on a representative sample of the Missouri Coteau of the northern Great Plains' mixed-grass prairie. As part of CCP implementation, Lostwood will be providing breeding habitat for up to 25 pairs of piping plover, and habitat for migrating bald eagle, peregrine falcon, and whooping crane.

EXPLANATION OF IMPACTS OF ACTION ON LISTED SPECIES OR CRITICAL HABITAT:

As part of CCP implementation, Lostwood will be providing breeding habitat for up to 25 pairs of piping plover, and habitat for migrating bald eagle, peregrine falcon, and whooping crane. The CCP includes the following endangered species goal and objectives:

> "**Endangered Species Goal:** To preserve, restore, and enhance indigenous flora and fauna that are candidate, threatened, endangered, or species of special interest.

>> **Objective A.** Maintain at least nine breeding pairs of piping plovers and increase, where possible, habitat to accommodate at least 16 additional breeding pairs, with a mean fledgling rate at least 1.2 young per breeding pair.

Strategies:
1. Monitor reproductive success of pairs through fledging to evaluate effects of management activities on piping plovers.
2. Maintain and improve shoreline habitat (e.g., prescribed burning, grazing, salt applications, gravel addition)
3. Protect beaches and nests from predators (e.g., by use of barrier fences)
4. Create new nesting beaches where appropriate

Objective B. Provide protection and habitat for the following migrant threatened and endangered species: peregrine falcon, bald eagle, and whooping crane.

Strategies:
1. Provide attractive shoreline habitats for shorebirds, a staple prey for migrating peregrine falcons
2. Provide roosting sites during fall for migrating snow geese, a staple prey for migrating bald eagles
3. Provide exposed shorelines and grazed or burned uplands for spring and fall migrating whooping cranes..."

CONCLUSION:

Implementation of the Comprehensive Conservation Plan for Lostwood National Wildlife Refuge will not adversely affect any threatened or endangered species: implementation should benefit both habitats and prey populations for listed species..

CONCURRENCE WITH CONCLUSION:

Acting GARD - RW-ND/SD

Aug. 14, 1998
Date

GARD - ES-MT/WY

8/17/98
Date

APPENDIX E

Summary of Public Involvement

The manager of Lostwood Refuge periodically discussed management practices with Federal, State, and local agencies. Various management practices are discussed with Natural Resource Conservation Service (NRCS) specialists for their professional input. The refuge manager is often consulted by other managers of state and Federal lands regarding habitat management practices, especially use of prescribed fire in managing native prairie and in reseeding native prairie grasses. The refuge manager has presented the results of Lostwood Refuge's successful leafy spurge control program to several groups over the past decade and has kept the County Weed Supervisors informed of the program. The Lostwood Communication Council consists of nine interested local individuals from Burke and Mountrail Counties. Meetings have been held three to six times per year to discuss management and plans for the Refuge, and answer local concerns over Refuge management. Local sportsmen's club meetings are attended as opportunities arise, and policies and management practices are explained.

The North Dakota Department of Health has been consulted over several years regarding the prescribed burning program. Of primary concern has been smoke management from prescribed fires. Lostwood Refuge also has worked cooperatively with the Health Department on studies of air quality.

A Waterfowl Planning Meeting for the Des Lacs National Wildlife Refuge Complex including Des Lacs and Lostwood Refuges and Lostwood and Crosby Wetland Management Districts was held in Crosby, North Dakota in September 1992. The MAAPE process (Multi-Agency Approach to Planning and Evaluation) was a planning effort directed to improve management practices on the Complex. Representatives from Federal and state conservation agencies and private conservation organizations attended this planning meeting and provided input.

Copies of the 1994 Environmental Assessment, entitled "Management of Upland Habitats on Lostwood National Wildlife Refuge," were mailed to all agencies and persons who had expressed interest in the management of the Refuge. Letters announcing the availability of the EA were sent to all members of the Lostwood Communication Council. News releases announcing the availability of the draft EA were published in local and regional newspapers. Only one comment (a letter of support) was received from the public during or after the 30-day comment period. A Notice of Decision was mailed to all persons who expressed an interest in receiving the Service's decision.

The Draft Comprehensive Management Plan was available for public review and comment from August 25 to September 30, 1997. In addition to the plan being sent to 115 people on the mailing list, news releases were provided to local and regional papers announcing the public review period and an open house was held on September 17, 1997, in Stanley, North Dakota. Approximately ten people attended the open house. The Service received 20 letters. Most respondents were supportive of the Plan. General comments were provided in the following categories:

Air quality clarification - 2
Against additional acquisition - 2
Comments concerning acquisition and mgmt of existing lands - 2
More upland game bird hunting if it won't affect wintering waterfowl - 1
Burn more - 1

Public comments/concerns have been addressed in the final Comprehensive Conservation Plan, except for those below:

The U.S. Fish and Wildlife Service and the National Wildlife Refuge System will comply with the Clean Air Act. In the Draft CMP, the authors did not include the number of burns and acres burned each year that may address some of the comments. From 1978-97, Lostwood Refuge averaged 3.8 prescribed burns and 2,410 acres per year from 1978-97 (range 1 [2 acres]-7 [2,466 acres] burns per year). From 1990-97, Lostwood Refuge averaged 3.5 prescribed burns and 3,160 acres per year from 1990-97 (range 1 [116 acres] to 6 [8,116 acres, includes wilderness burns]).

The Service is trying to take a holistic approach in management of the Wilderness Area, for without grazing, fire and rest, we will not be able to preserve the natural and biological values of the wilderness area. The air and water quality of this system is all part of the holistic approach.

The 1997-98 CCP for Lostwood Refuge has no significant change from the EA, even though the CCP is more comprehensively addressing wetland management, cultural resources, public use, and research. Wetland management is part of upland management because the many closed-system wetlands are interspersed in the uplands. Objectives for Lostwood Refuge were first addressed and published in a 1971 "Master Plan." These were further developed and expanded in the Goals and Objectives in the Operating Statement approved in September 1991. The Draft CMP further developed and expanded these goals and objectives, and have no significant change to the long-term policy, mission, and management of the Refuge because of the EA.

APPENDIX F

Mailing List of Agencies and Individuals

FEDERAL OFFICIALS
* U.S. Senator Kent Conrad
  Gail Bergstad, State Representative, Minot, ND
* U.S. Senator Bryon L. Dorgan
  Bob Valeu, State Coordinator, Bismarck, ND
* U.S. Representative Earl Pomeroy
  Gail Skaley, State Director, Bismarck, ND

FEDERAL AGENCIES
* USDA/Natural Resources Conservation Service, Lincoln, NE
* USGS/Biological Resources Div., Jamestown, ND
* USGS/Biological Resources Div., Ft. Collins, CO
* USDI/Bureau of Land Management, Billings, MT
* USDI/Bureau of Reclamation, Billings, MT
* USDI/Bureau of Indian Affairs, Billings, MT
* U.S. Army Corps of Engineers, St. Paul, MN; Williston, ND
* Environmental Protection Agency, Denver, CO
* USDI/National Park Service, Theodore Roosevelt National Park, Medora, ND
* USDI/Fish and Wildlife Service, Denver, CO; Bismarck, ND; Anchorage, AK; Portland, OR; Albuquerque, NM; Fort Snelling, MN; Atlanta, GA; Hadley, MA; Washington, D.C.
* USDI/Fish and Wildlife Service, Ecological Services Office, Bismarck, ND
* USDI/Fish and Wildlife Service, Minot Wetlands Acquisition Office, Minot, ND
* Air Quality Branch, Lakewood, CO

STATE OFFICIALS
* Governor Edward T. Schafer, Bismarck, ND
* Senator John Andrist, Crosby, ND
* Senator Meyer Kinnoin, Palermo, ND
* Representative Glen Froseth, Kenmare, ND
* Representative Ronald Nichols, Palermo, ND
* Representative Robert Skarphol, Tioga, ND
* Representative Torgie Torgenson, Ray, ND
* Representative John Warner, Ryder, ND

STATE AGENCIES
* North Dakota Game and Fish Department, Bismarck, ND
* Missouri River Natural Resources Committee, Bismarck, ND
* State Engineer, Bismarck, ND
* State Historical Society of North Dakota, Bismarck, ND

CITY/COUNTY/LOCAL GOVERNMENTS
* Mayor, City of Kenmare
* City Council, City of Kenmare
* Mayor, City of Stanley
* City Council, City of Stanley
* Burke County Commissioner, Bowbells, ND
* Burke County Commissioner, Powers Lake, ND
* Burke County Commissioner, Columbus, ND
* Cass County Land Department, Baukus, MN
* Mountrail County Commissioner, Stanley, ND
* Mountrail County Commissioner, Stanley, ND

NATIVE AMERICAN TRIBES
* Three Affiliated Tribe Business Council, New Town, ND

FIRE DEPARTMENTS
* Kenmare Fire Department, Kenmare, ND
* Bowbells Fire Department, Bowbells, ND
* Stanley Fire Department, Stanley, ND
* Powers Lake Fire Department, Powers Lake, ND

ORGANIZATIONS/BUSINESS/CIVIC GROUPS
* Cooperative Alliance for Refuge Enhancement (CARE), Washington, D.C.
* National Wildlife Refuge Association, Denver, CO
* American Birding Association, Colorado Springs, CO
* The Wildlife Society, North Dakota Chapter, Bismarck, ND
* American Fisheries Society, Dakota Chapter, Pierre, SD
* North Dakota Wildlife Federation, Bismarck, ND
* Ducks Unlimited, Inc., Bismarck, ND
* Defenders of Wildlife, Missoula, MT
* Sierra Club Northern Plains Field Office, Sheridan, WY
* The Nature Conservancy, Helena, MT
* Environmental Defense Fund, Boulder, CO
* Prairie Wetlands Resource Center, Bismarck, ND
* Pheasants Forever, Inc., Huron, SD
* Native American Fish and Wildlife Society, Broomfield, CO
* Great Plains Partnership, Western Governors Association, Denver, CO
* Central Flyway Council, Saskatoon, Saskatchewan
* Dickinson Research Center, Dickinson, ND
* Lostwood Farms, Ltd., Stanley, ND
* Bluestem Company, Bismarck, ND
* Canadian Wildlife Society, Edmonton, Alberta, Canada

NEWSPAPERS
* The Kenmare News, Kenmare, ND
* Mountrail County Promoter, Stanley, ND
* Burke County Tribune, Bowbells, ND
* Williston Daily Herald, Williston, ND
* Minot Daily News, Minot, ND

UNIVERSITIES/COLLEGES/SCHOOLS
* South Dakota State University, Brookings, SD
* University of North Dakota, Grand Forks, ND
* University of Minnesota, Crookston, MN
* Minot State University, Minot, ND
* University of Minnesota, St. Paul, MN
* University of Missouri-Columbia, Columbia, MO
* Department of Biology, Montana State University, Bozeman, MT
* MT Coop. Wildlife, University of Montana, Missoula, MT
* Powers Lake Public School

INDIVIDUALS
Anderson, Keith and Sharon
Biwer, Neal and Cherlyn
Berkey, Gordon
Cornatzer, Dr. William
Dailey, Paulette
Edwards, Lee and Diane
Graff, Becky
Green, Dr. Mike
Higgins, Ken
Kallberg, Grant
Kallberg, Keith
Kruse, Arnold
Lindberg, Clinton
Lindberg, Dennis
Lucy, Agnes
Lucy, Jack
Madden, Beth
Martin, Ron
Paul, Gary and Marsha
Smith, Clayton
Stewart, John and Betty
Tinjum, Larry
Vaage, Lowell and Corraine
Van Berkom, Steve
Walks, Sharon
Wilde, Jon

APPENDIX G

Preparers and Acknowledgments

Karen Smith: Preface, Introduction and Background, Plan Implementation, Subsection: Habitat Protection Strategy

Robert Murphy, Dan Severson, Karen Smith: Resource and Refuge Description, Refuge Goals and Objectives, Subsections: Purpose and Regulatory Statutes, Establishment and History, Ecological Setting and Description, Environment Assessment, Mission, Goals, Objectives, and Strategies

Editing was completed by Robert Murphy

Mapping completed by Jaymee Fojtik, USFWS, Denver, CO

Desktop publishing completed by Barbara Shupe and Melvie Uhland, USFWS, Denver, CO

APPENDIX H

Key Legislation/Policies

In implementing the Comprehensive Conservation Plan, the Service will comply with the following Federal Laws and Executive Orders.

Antiquities Act (1906): Authorizes the scientific investigation of antiquities on Federal land and provides penalties for unauthorized removal of objects taken or collected without a permit.

Migratory Bird Treaty Act (1918): Designates the protection of migratory birds as a Federal responsibility. This Act enables the setting of seasons, and other regulations including the closing of areas, Federal or non-Federal to the hunting of migratory birds.

Migratory Bird Conservation Act (1929): Establishes procedures for acquisition by purchase, rental, or gift of areas approved by the Migratory Bird Conservation Commission.

Migratory Bird Hunting and Conservation Stamp Act (1934): Authorized the opening of part of a refuge to waterfowl hunting.

Fish and Wildlife Act (1956): Established a comprehensive national fish and wildlife policy and broadened the authority for acquisition and development of refuges.

Fish and Wildlife Coordination Act (1958): Allows the Fish and Wildlife Service to enter into agreements with private landowners for wildlife management purposes.

Refuge Recreation Act (1962): Allows the use of refuges for recreation when such uses are compatible with the refuge's primary purposes and when sufficient funds are available to manage the uses.

Land and Water Conservation Fund Act (1965): Uses the receipts from the sale of surplus Federal land, outer continental shelf oil and gas sales, and other sources for land acquisition under several authorities.

Wilderness Act of 1964: Required the Secretary of the Interior to review roadless areas of 5,000 acres or more and all roadless islands within the National Wildlife Refuge System, and to recommend areas for inclusion in the National Wilderness Preservation System. Final decisions on wilderness are made by Congress.

National Wildlife Refuge System Administration Act (1966): Defines the National Wildlife Refuge System and authorizes the Secretary to permit any use of a refuge provided such use is compatible with the major purposes for which the refuge was established.

National Historic Preservation Act (1966) as amended: Establishes as policy that the Federal Government is to provide leadership in the preservation of the nation's prehistoric and historic resources.

Architectural Barriers Act (1968): Requires federally owned, leased, or funded buildings and facilities to be accessible to persons with disabilities.

National Environmental Policy Act (1969): Requires the disclosure of the environmental impacts of any major Federal action significantly affecting the quality of the human environment.

Endangered Species Act (1973): Requires all Federal agencies to carry out programs for the conservation of endangered and threatened species.

Rehabilitation Act (1973): Requires programmatic accessibility in addition to physical accessibility for all facilities and programs funded by the Federal government to ensure that anybody can participate in any program.

Archaeological and Historic Preservation Act (1974): Directs the preservation of historic and archaeological data in Federal construction projects.

Clean Air Act: Establishes requirements to prevent significant deterioration of air quality, and in particular, to preserve air quality in national parks, national wilderness areas, national monuments, and national seashores.

Clean Water Act (1977): Requires consultation with the Corps of Engineers (404 permits) for major wetland modifications.

Executive Order 11988 (1977): Each Federal agency shall provide leadership and take action to reduce the risk of flood loss and minimize the impact of floods on human safety, and preserve the natural and beneficial values served by the floodplains.

American Indian Religious Freedom Act (1978): Directs agencies to consult with native traditional religious leaders to determine appropriate policy changes necessary to protect and preserve Native American religious cultural rights and practices.

Archaeological Resources Protection Act (1979) as amended: Protects materials of archaeological interest from unauthorized removal or destruction and requires Federal managers to develop plans and schedules to locate archaeological resources.

Emergency Wetlands Resources Act (1986): The purpose of the Act is "To promote the conservation of migratory waterfowl and to offset or prevent the serious loss of wetlands by the acquisition of wetlands and other essential habitat, and for other purposes."

Federal Noxious Weed Act (1990): Requires the use of integrated management systems to control or contain undesirable plant species; and an interdisciplinary approach with the cooperation of other Federal and State agencies.

Native American Graves Protection and Repatriation Act (1990): Requires Federal agencies and museums to inventory, determine ownership of, and repatriate cultural items under their control or possession.

Americans With Disabilities Act (1992): Prohibits discrimination in public accommodations and services.

Executive Order 12996 Management and General Public Use of the National Wildlife Refuge System (1996): Defines the mission, purpose, and priority public uses of the National Wildlife Refuge System. It also presents four principles to guide management of the Refuge System.

Executive Order 13007 Indian Sacred Sites (1996): Directs Federal land management agencies to accommodate access to and ceremonial use of Indian sacred sites by Indian religious practitioners, avoid adversely affecting the physical integrity of such sacred sites, and where appropriate, maintain the confidentiality of sacred sites.

National Wildlife Refuge System Improvement Act of 1997: Clearly defines a unifying mission for the Refuge System; establishes the legitimacy and appropriateness of the six priority public uses (hunting, fishing, wildlife observation and photography, or environmental education and interpretation); establishes a formal process for determining compatibility; establishes the responsibilities of the Secretary of Interior for managing and protecting the System; and requires a Comprehensive Conservation Plan for each refuge by the year 2012. This Act amended portions of the Refuge Recreation Act and National Wildlife Refuge System Administration Act of 1966.

APPENDIX I

Reference Maps

Map 5

Map 6.

APPENDIX J

Executive Order Establishing Lostwood Refuge

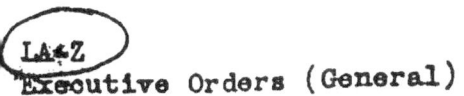
Executive Order

ESTABLISHING LOSTWOOD MIGRATORY WATERFOWL REFUGE

NORTH DAKOTA

By virtue of and pursuant to the authority vested in me as President of the United States, and in order to effectuate further the purposes of the Migratory Bird Conservation Act (45 Stat. 1222), it is ordered that the following-described lands, acquired or to be acquired by the United States, in Burke and Mountrail Counties, North Dakota, consisting of 33,045 acres, more or less, be, and they are hereby, reserved and set apart for the use of the Department of Agriculture, subject to valid existing rights, as a refuge and breeding ground for migratory birds and other wild life: *Provided*, That any private lands within the areas described shall become a part of the refuge hereby established upon the acquisition of title or lease thereto by the United States:

FIFTH PRINCIPAL MERIDIAN

T. 158 N., R. 91 W., secs. 3 to 10, inclusive;
secs. 17 to 20, inclusive.
T. 159 N., R. 91 W., secs. 3 to 10, inclusive;
secs. 15 to 18, inclusive;
secs. 20, 21, and 22;
sec. 26, NW¼SW¼;
secs. 27, 28, and 29;
secs. 32, 33, and 34.
T. 160 N., R. 91 W., secs. 19 to 23, inclusive;
secs. 25 to 35, inclusive.
T. 158 N., R. 92 W., secs. 13 and 24.
T. 159 N., R. 92 W., secs. 11 to 14, inclusive.

This refuge shall be known as the Lostwood Migratory Waterfowl Refuge.

FRANKLIN D ROOSEVELT

THE WHITE HOUSE,
September 4, 1935.

[No. 7171]

APPENDIX K

Plant Species

Appendix list of dominant spp present on Lostwood Refuge.

Xeric sites: needle-and-thread (Stipa comata), plains muhly (Muhlenbergia cuspidata), blue grama (Bouteloua gracillis), and prairie junegrass (Koeleria pyramidata).

Slope sites: western wheatgrass (Agronpyron smithii), rough fescue (Festuca scabrella), green needlegrass (Stipa viridula), Pennsylvania sedge (Carex pennsylvanica), early bluegrass (Poa cusickii).

Mesic sites: big bluestem (Andropogon gerardi), prairie cordgrass (Spartina pectinata), mat muhly (Muhlenbergia richardsonis), and prairie dropseed (Sporobolus heterolepis).

Native forbs composition will include purple coneflower (Echinacea angustifolia), blanketflower (Gaillardia aristata), wild onion (Allium spp.), Canada anemone (Anemone canadensis), smallflower aster (Aster falactus), smooth blue aster (A. laevis), milkvetches (Astragalus spp.), fleabanes (Erigeron spp.), Liatrises (Liatris spp.), and northern bedstraw (Galium boreale).

Lostwood National Wildlife Refuge
8315 Highway 8
Kenmare, ND 58746
701/848 2722
r6rw_lst@fws.gov

U. S. Fish and Wildlife Service
http://www.fws.gov

For Refuge Information
1 800/344 WILD

December 1998

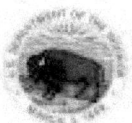